ACTION
FOR LIFE!

12 SECRETS FOR CREATING
YOUR BEST LIFE

Kristin Blair Wnuk

Copyright © 2008 by Kristin Blair Wnuk

All rights reserved. No part of this book shall be reproduced or transmitted in any form or by any means, electronic, mechanical, magnetic, photographic including photocopying, recording or by any information storage and retrieval system, without prior written permission of the publisher. No patent liability is assumed with respect to the use of the information contained herein. Although every precaution has been taken in the preparation of this book, the publisher and author assume no responsibility for errors or omissions. Neither is any liability assumed for damages resulting from the use of the information contained herein.

ISBN 0-7414-4502-6

Cover Photography: Marty Allen Photography
Cover Design: Joel Storey www.joelstorey.com

Published by:

INFINITY
PUBLISHING.COM

1094 New DeHaven Street, Suite 100
West Conshohocken, PA 19428-2713
Info@buybooksontheweb.com
www.buybooksontheweb.com
Toll-free (877) BUY BOOK
Local Phone (610) 941-9999
Fax (610) 941-9959

Printed in the United States of America
Printed on Recycled Paper
Published February 2008

To my husband, Rick, and the three shining stars of my life: Alec, Jake, and Natalia—thank you for lighting up my life with your radiance.
You inspire me each and every day.

Table of Contents

Acknowledgments — i

Preface — iii

Introduction — 1

Chapter 1 — 11
Personal Foundation: Know Where You Are.

Chapter 2 — 27
Take Action. Life Expands Through Risk.
    The Law of Action — 28

Chapter 3 — 47
You and Only You Are Responsible for Your Life.
    The Law of Expectations — 48
    The Law of Responsibility — 64

Chapter 4 — 77
There is Always a Choice.
    The Law of Choices — 78
    The Law of Integrity — 79

Chapter 5 — 101
Embrace Unique. Embrace Your Authentic Self.
    The Law of Compassion — 105

Chapter 6 — 137
There Are No Mistakes, Only Opportunities to Learn
    The Law of Perfection — 142

Chapter 7	161
Attitude is Everything. Live In Gratitude.	
The Law of Gratitude	169
Chapter 8	189
Acknowledge Progress and Celebrate Victories.	
The Law of Process	195
Chapter 9	217
Seek to Create Meaningful Communication	
The Law of Flexibility	221
Chapter 10	251
Attract What You Want with the Right Mindset	
The Law of Abundance	252
The Law of Attraction	260

Acknowledgments

I want to thank my family for your love, support, and encouragement to move forward with this dream. Thank you for being cheerleaders, mentors, and editors. To Maryann Blair, my mom, thank you for your limitless love and support. You have been my rock, my strength, and my friend. To Don Cox, my dad, thank you for all that you have taught me along the way. I am so grateful that you are part of my life.

I want to express my deepest thanks to all of the personal growth authors that have gone before me. Your words and wisdom have inspired me throughout my life.

I would also like to share my gratitude for the Fearless Living Institute. I am grateful for receiving outstanding training. To Rhonda Britten, thank you for pushing me to spread my own wings. I am grateful to Leslie Becker, my powerful partner; Carie Leung, a true friend and confidante; the outspoken ladies on my Leadership Team, and to all of the friends that I made throughout my journey with Fearless Living. Thank you to Cynthia Seely and Susie Peterson, my personal mentor coaches.

I am grateful to Kathleen Brennan, Mary Doria, Hoa Phan, and Nancy Lewis for participating in my group discussions week after week with so much honesty. Thank you to Jana Davis for believing in my abilities and to Maureen McVail for your editing support. Thank you to Julie Schmit, LeAnn Fitch, and Karen Hardin—I know I can always reach out to you, my dearest, lifelong friends. You are all beautiful, inspiring women.

To Bart Queen, you are incredibly gifted. Thanks for all you do.

I am grateful to the team at Infinity Publishing for your guidance and support.

Thank you to my extraordinary clients, past and present. You shine brightly and inspire me. Thank you for sharing all of who you are with me. I am honored that you chose me to be your Life Coach.

Preface

A few years ago, I faced a health crisis that was a great teacher in my life. As I recovered from that event, my life changed in ways I never could have imagined. I looked at my life differently. I could see with clarity how my thoughts, my self perceptions, and my fears influenced my life. I had a good life, but I wanted a great life, an authentic life. I wanted to wake up everyday with passion and excitement for the possibilities of a new day. I wanted to live with zest, enthusiasm, and a fearless spirit.

As I began implementing a few key strategies in my life, I could see that all that I needed was within me—I just needed to access it. In order to do that, I needed to make the choice to live by my values, on purpose, with purpose, each and every day. I needed to release thoughts that were disempowering and led me to doubt myself. I realized that it was time to be true to who I am and what I felt inside. It was time to trust myself and follow my heart.

In many ways, I feel like I have been a Life Coach my whole life. As far back as I can remember, I have been fascinated by people and what makes them tick. I have read countless books on behavior, leadership, self-esteem…you name it. For my friends, I was the voice of reason. Yet, despite having so much knowledge about why people do what they do, there was much for me to learn about applying what I knew to my life.

I saw myself as very driven, successful, and balanced between my work and family life. Yet, I did not make my health a priority and I had very high, unrealistic expectations of myself. I learned that there is a huge difference between conceptually knowing something and applying it to my life through action. I learned that "why" was not as important as "how". The understanding of why I got to where I am did not change my circumstances, so I learned to surrender to my present conditions by accepting the reality of the moment—it does not necessarily matter why I am here, as long as I learn something from this experience. This is the reality of my situation. The real question is, how am I going to create the life that I want?

As I went through my personal journey, I made a list of keys that I felt were critical to achieving a fulfilling life. These keys were the foundation for moving my life into a new direction and an empowered way of thinking. Interestingly enough, after I formulated my personal philosophy, I uncovered Life Laws that supported each of my personal keys.

Life Laws are a constant in life, just as the Law of Gravity is in physics. If we dropped an object from a tall building, we would not question where the object would go because we understand the forces of gravity. We cannot touch, smell, or see gravity, but we know that it is a constant force in our lives. The energy of Life Laws acts in the same way. Their energy is ever present. Each of our lives is governed by these laws, whether we recognize it or not, just as we are governed by gravity.

As I said, my life changed in ways I could never have imagined. I also noticed that the majority of my clients faced the same challenges that I faced. Their life circumstances or topics may have been different, but the underlying concepts were the same. Thus, the keys for my "Personal Philosophy for Life Success" and the supporting Life Laws became the foundation for the chapters in this book. These keys have supported my growth, the growth of my clients, and now I hope they will support you in the same way. To me, there is nothing more extraordinary than the power of the human spirit living fully. This book comes from my heart and is my gift to you, so that you too can live your life to its fullest.

This book incorporates simple concepts that when applied to your life can stimulate profound change and unlimited power. Each chapter contains specific exercises and questions that will support you in creating the life of your dreams. Each of us is unique and has our own life path. This book is designed to support you in uncovering what is holding you back, deciding to take action in a new way, and enabling you to live your best life. Here are the keys that changed my life:

> Kristin's Personal Philosophy for Success:
> - Personal Foundation: Get real about where you are.
> - Take action. Life expands through risk.
> - You and only you are responsible for your life.
> - There is always a choice.
> - Embrace unique. Discover your authentic self.
> - There are no mistakes, only opportunities to learn.
> - Attitude is everything. Find gratitude everywhere.
> - Acknowledge progress and celebrate victories.
> - Seek to create meaningful communication.
> - Attract what you want with the right mindset.

Introduction:

My Journey from Fear to Authenticity

Who am I? I always thought I had a very clear picture of who I am. When I would reflect, I knew who I was to the depths of my soul. Yet, was that the person that I shared with the world? When I thought I was going through life being me, was I really being me? In truth, I lived my life floating back and forth in a complex dance between fear and freedom. The free me was the true me, the beautiful, loving, joyous human soul I was created to be. The fearful me, I created based on my perceptions of how I should show up in the world in order to be accepted. I thought the fearful me was a secret, someone I kept hidden inside myself. That was the side of me I didn't share with anyone else. The fearful me was far too vulnerable to expose to the world. If I was going to get anywhere in this world, I had to make sure that the confident, motivated, upbeat side of me was what people saw.

I love people. In fact, I have always been fascinated by them. I have often wondered what made me do the things I do and what made others do what they do? Was I alone with my secret fears or did everyone else have them too? Was I being my true self or was my fear fooling me? I have always seen myself as a little different from everyone else, as someone who didn't quite fit in with the crowd. Despite having my secret fears, I excelled in my life. I worked hard and strived for excellence. Or was it perfection?

One area of my life always felt a little more challenging to me. I longed for deeper connections with people. I spent a lot of time being the new kid and I was relatively shy. It seemed I never knew quite what to say, so I'd often silently stand on the sidelines and smile so that people would at least know I was friendly. Sometimes, I felt invisible and other times, silence was so uncomfortable, I would speak at warp speed in a nonsensical way. I chose my friends very carefully. It seemed that many females were intentionally competitive with each other instead of supportive of one another. So I was drawn to people I sensed I could trust. When I trusted someone, I knew I could be myself. If that trust was broken, however, I was devastated. I recoiled back into myself. I was safer on my own. I knew I had flaws and imperfections. I thought people would be disappointed in my flaws, so I tried to cover them up. I bought into the pictures of the perfect people hanging out with their perfect friends and families taking the perfect vacations and sharing the perfect holidays. Almost on an unconscious level, I adopted this as my standard.

When I was 14 years old, my father asked me what I wanted to do with my life. Of course, I was not really sure (because I lived in my questions). I answered as honestly as I could: "I'm not sure, but I know I want to help people." I will never forget the look of disappointment on my father's face. Don't get me wrong, my father is a hard working, self-made man and a good man. He wanted the best for me and he wanted me to live up to my potential. I interpreted his look one way and he meant it another way. It was an off of the cuff moment that we didn't really talk about, but it stayed with me. I wanted the people I loved to be proud of me, but I did not know then that just being me was all I needed to be.

"Who am I?" haunted me. I felt like there was this disconnect between who I was and who I thought I should be. I felt like I had a strong character, but I still had that nagging feeling that somehow I wasn't enough. I was not tall enough or pretty enough or thin enough or smart enough or funny enough or kind enough or friendly enough. I was not sure if I could measure up to whom I was supposed to be or what society expected of me. The "me" I projected to the world seemed confident and focused, but on the inside I felt like a fraud.

After graduating from college, I pursued a career in sales. A few years later, I married a great guy, had three children, and settled into a picturesque life in suburbia. I felt very content because I had all of the things in my life that I thought I wanted. The nagging question of "Who am I?" seemed to be answered. I was a sales professional, a wife, a mother, a volunteer, a friend, a daughter, and a sister. I created a very full and busy life, a life that I was proud of. I had many admirable roles. It was my perceptions of my life, not my life itself, that were leading me to disaster.

Somewhere along the way, I learned that one of the easiest ways for me to connect with people was by being seen as adding value to their lives. It became an almost unconscious response or state of being. I would discount my own needs in order to fulfill someone else's needs. I thought I was being caring. I would discount my own thoughts to keep the peace. I thought I was being the bigger person. I became extremely talented at seeing each person's side of an issue and I was a great team player. I saw myself as gifted because I could anticipate other people's needs. Taking care of myself was not a priority for me in any way, shape, or form. I was the one with the positive attitude, the upbeat personality, and the "I can do it" mantra. I saw myself as being the one to motivate others. When I didn't feel well, I pretended I was fine or I isolated myself so that no one would know. I liked people counting on me and seeing me as someone who related well to others. I did not know that my secret fears were at work.

There were many parts of my life that were really wonderful. The creative side of me loved decorating my home or planning parties. The loving side of me enjoyed spending time with my beautiful family. The competitive side of me reveled in the thrill of achieving my sales goals. The adventurous side of me talked my husband into taking a risk and moving to another state. On the outside, I looked like I was living the American Dream.

After the birth of my third child, my perceptions started to catch up with me. I had a complicated pregnancy and was on bed rest for several months before she was born. Being in bed was pure torture for me. It was a wake up call that I did not hear. I wanted to get up and "do". I wanted to feel productive. The love I had for my unborn baby kept me in bed, but as a person I was miserable. I laid in bed, cried, and ate for the last three months of my pregnancy. After my daughter was born, I had a 4 year old, a 3 year old, a newborn, and 85 pounds to lose. To make my life even more interesting, when I returned to work, I found out that my sales territory had been realigned. I went from being a top sales representative, who had won numerous awards, to a bottom feeder. I took it like a champ and got to work. I knew I wouldn't allow myself to be there for long. I was a winner and winners always rise to the top.

I was in hospital sales and hospitals are open 24 hours a day. I worked around the clock in order to get my sales numbers up. I saw myself as the Go-To-Gal at work. I made it clear that if my boss or my team needed something from me, I was there in full force. Letting someone down or being a disappointment was not an option. I did not realize it then, but my worth as a person was tied to it.

I was dieting, exercising like a mad woman to lose the baby weight. I was working around the clock. I was getting up with my kids at night and trying to be Super Mom. Something had to give.

After months of pushing myself to my limits, I began to experience symptoms of intense fatigue. I fought it for a while and then finally went to see a doctor. The doctor explained to me that because I was a working mother of three children who was trying to lose weight, I should not expect to have energy. The doctor sent me on my way and I continued living my life and doing what I had always done.

My health spiraled downward. I changed jobs hoping that a less demanding job would alleviate some of the stress in my life. It did not work. I started having more intense symptoms and chronic bronchitis developed. I knew something was very wrong with me and doctor after doctor treated me as if it was all in my head. Even after I got a decent amount of sleep, I was so exhausted during the day that I could barely keep my eyes open. I craved sugar and caffeine because they were the only things I could count on to keep me going. As a sales representative, I spent a great deal of time on the road. I caught myself falling asleep at the wheel several times and I knew something had to change.

My husband and I had built our lifestyle on two incomes. I had always planned to work. I never planned on getting sick. I felt like I would be letting him down if I walked away from my career. I was afraid of falling apart financially. Our home was filled with stress. I was always exhausted and always on edge. I knew I was not the person that I wanted to be, but I did not have enough energy to be anyone else. Months went by and I soldiered on. I saw more doctors and they suggested I just take an antidepressant and keep going. I felt sick, tired, lost, and alone.

After having a nasty case of pneumonia and several rounds of bronchitis, I resigned from my job. It was such a painful decision for me. I felt ashamed for not being able to handle what every other working mother could handle. I felt selfish for needing to take care of myself. I felt a sense of loss because my identity as a top sales representative was gone. The negative voice in my head shouted that I am a worthless failure. I kept telling myself that after a few months of rest, I would get back to work and be my normal, energetic, driven self. That did not happen.

I would wake up in the morning and feel a little energy, just enough to get my kids ready and out the door to school and daycare. By 10:00 am, the fatigue was so overwhelming that I could not stay awake. I was plagued by dizziness, heart palpitations, low blood pressure, cravings for salt and sugar, muscle weakness, and chronic chest infections. I could not think clearly and my memory seemed to just disappear. I would sleep all day, because I could not keep myself awake. Then, the depression really set in. It was deep and overwhelming. It was by far the darkest time of my life. I would lay in bed all day, everyday and sleep, sometimes for 15 hours. When I was awake, I would cry and cry and cry. I could not break free of the sadness, no matter how hard I tried. Worst of all, I did not know how to get better. I still did not have a doctor that believed me. I even hid my symptoms as much as I could from my husband. I guess I was trying to spare myself from the look of disappointment on his face as well. I was sure he felt like he was the victim of "bait and switch". I was no longer the person he married.

Everything that I perceived that I contributed to the world was now gone. I could not be a productive member of society. I could not be a good wife or mother to my children. My career was over. I could not get out of bed long enough to even clean up my house. I could barely take care of myself much less anyone else. Even the smallest task drained me. I felt worthless. At night, I would talk to God and ask him to take me in my sleep because I believed my family would be better off without me. I thought I was a useless, unproductive burden. That was the depression talking. The negative voice in my head screamed endlessly at me. How could I have done this to myself? A horrible disease like cancer did not do this to me, I did this! I chose not to take care of myself. I chose to live with chronic, intense stress. I created this. What kind of awful person could do this to the people she loves?

After about a year of sleeping and beating myself up, I found a flicker of my authentic self, my real self. I began to research all of my symptoms on the internet. It was not the best way to figure out what was wrong with me, but it was the only thing left for me to try. I came across a book on adrenal disorders and the symptoms fit. I bought the book, began implementing all of the suggestions, and with lots of rest, started to make small steps toward getting better. My thinking got clearer which helped me immensely. I could see with more clarity that the negative thinking and beating myself up were not helping me. I decided that I would celebrate every small step forward. If I was able to get up, make dinner and do the dishes, I celebrated and congratulated myself. If I was able to stay awake for three hours straight instead of two hours, I told myself that I am amazing! I knew I had to turn off my negative voice and turn on my self-loving voice.

I finally found a doctor that did some tests and confirmed an adrenal and thyroid disorder. With his help, I was able to make physical progress much faster. It was a very long, tedious, and often frustrating road back to health. Yet, I was deeply grateful to be on that road. While healing my body, I recognized that I needed to take a hard look at myself to figure out what it was about me that brought me to adrenal exhaustion in the first place.

I had never really seen myself as someone whose fear was in control. After all, I had gone skydiving. I had been bold at an interview and landed the job of my dreams. I had bought a book of the fifty best places to raise a family and talked my husband into relocating. I had decided that my front porch needed a face lift, so I went to the store, got supplies and directions, and laid cement all by myself. I was fiercely independent. I believed that I could do pretty much anything I set my mind to. I thought I had buried the fearful side of me and I believed that I was fearless.

The internal exploration began. Being needed is great, right? Everyone wants to be valued. What was it about me that took it to an extreme? It was fear. I loved being needed by others, but I was not willing to need anyone else. I could be caring and loving to others, but I rarely let people cross that line to be there for me. It was always in the back of my mind that people could walk out of my life, so I convinced myself that I had to stay in a position of always being willing to let a relationship go. It was my way of avoiding rejection and loss. Needing someone else was excruciatingly uncomfortable. If I relied on myself, I stayed emotionally safe. I had a very deep seeded fear of rejection and loss. Fear of rejection also caused me to put my thoughts, feelings, and needs last. I over apologized when it was not my fault. I rationalized my actions as being considerate of others, but the truth was I was afraid to put myself first. Fear was the reason I did not take care of my body. I made everything and everyone else more important. If I was not there for everyone, I would not be needed. If I was not needed, I would feel rejected. It made me a great listener and a great team player, but I was not acting from an empowered or healthy place.

Fear had control in my life in so many subtle ways. I was very good at covering it up. When I finally shared my secrets, so many people who knew me were surprised. Worrying is fear. Assuming I knew what other people think about me is fear. Not giving myself a break, doubting myself, and not asking for help when I knew I needed it are all fear based responses. Keeping my guard up, isolating myself, and basing my value on what I could do instead of who I am are all fear. Fear of rejection and looking foolish kept me from connecting; fear of letting others down kept me on my personal hamster wheel; fear of what others would think kept me trying to keep up a facade of perfection. I compared myself to other women. I had unrealistic standards. I lived my life by all of the things I thought I "should" do to be a success in life. Once I recognized my fears, I was able to radically change my thoughts and my behaviors. Just noticing how fear showed up in my life was profoundly important. My first big awareness was that all of my fears started with a thought, a thought that I created based upon my perceptions. Changing my thoughts has changed my world. My comfort zone was rejecting my own thoughts, feelings, and needs in order to feel valued. I changed my thoughts, took new action and today, my life is a joyous journey.

Instead of living in a mad frenzy trying to get somewhere or prove something, I now choose to live my life in a whole new way. I feel centered and peaceful. I find gifts in every experience. I have a clear sense of purpose. I live my life with intention by consciously choosing to take action based upon what I value as a person. I choose to be a patient, mentor to my kids. I ask for help and accept help. I take care of myself, nurturing my spirit and my body. I wake up excited for the day. I love everything about my life. I love sharing who I am. I love connecting with people. I love sharing my journey with other people and supporting them in living their best life and finding their freedom. The joy, exuberance, and confidence are genuine because they come from the authentic me.

My desire to help people has now come full circle. I have found my passion and my purpose. I share my experience, my love of people, and my desire to help in an empowering way. I give of my true self, my free self, my beautiful self, not of my fearful self. Every single thing I have experienced in my life has brought me to where I am today and I wouldn't change a thing. My experiences and diverse back ground give me a unique perspective. I used my experience, enhanced my skills, went through additional training, and followed my dream to become a Certified Life Coach. My journey has been such a gift and it has taught me so much. By being true to myself, I have found my best life. I want to share with you the secrets of living your best life, mastering fear, and taking action to create the life of your dreams.

All of my best to you,
Kristin Blair Wnuk

Chapter 1

Personal Foundation: Know Where You Are.

"The greatest revolution of my life is the discovery that individuals can change the outer aspects of their lives by changing the inner attitudes of their minds."

—William James

The reality of life is that we all have choices, no matter our circumstances. The premise of this book is to help you create the life that you really want. It shares Life Laws, tools, and exercises, that once applied and practiced, can change your life immediately. These principles or Life Laws have been around for centuries and by simply incorporating them into your thinking and actions, you can make drastic changes starting today...

What do you really want for your life? What would it mean to you to feel stress free, centered, excited and happy throughout your life? How would your life change if you felt passionate about what you are doing everyday? What would it mean to you to pursue your dreams without allowing your fears to stop you? Imagine feeling alive with a zest for life, having meaningful relationships, sincere self-confidence and self-trust, and a belief that anything is possible for you. Anything *is* possible for you. You can have everything you want in your life.

Everything that we do, believe, feel, and choose in our lives begins with our thoughts. Everything. Everything we are or ever will be is determined by the expansiveness or limitation of our thoughts. Our thoughts create our reality by stimulating the actions that we take. They determine our belief systems. They create our emotions and our emotions influence our actions. If we are feeling inner peace, it is because we are having peaceful thoughts. If we are feeling frustrated, our thoughts are focused on something that is not happening the way we want it to. Our thoughts create our responses to the world. They create our dreams, goals, and fears. Our thoughts are at the root of everything we know, believe, feel, and experience in our lives. So, if we change our thoughts, we can change our feelings, actions, and ultimately our life? Absolutely!

When we want to make a change in our life, we usually want to change how we feel or what we do. Yet, in order to change our feelings or actions, we must start by changing our minds. Changing your inner experiences, perceptions, and thoughts will change how you experience life in the real world. It requires making a choice, committing to that choice, and then taking action. I have found with my coaching clients that this concept sometimes takes time to fully understand and integrate into their lives. Once it happens, they see profound changes.

Many of us want to believe that we are victims of our circumstances in some way, shape, or form. We have a boss that is unreasonable; we have suffered a tragedy; we have parents that hold us back; or we have responsibilities that use up all of our time. We all have choices, no matter what our circumstances. We get to decide how we handle every challenge and every opportunity that comes our way. No one else is responsible for making us do anything. No one else is responsible for making us feel anything. These are our choices and ours alone. Yes, our lives are influenced by our environments, childhoods, and cultural beliefs. Yet, we each have the opportunity to make choices as to what we are willing to welcome into our lives and what we want to reject from our lives and our belief systems. We have the power to change our thoughts. We have the power to change our habits, our actions, and our responses to everything that happens in our lives.

> *The reality is we all have choices, no matter our circumstances.*

We each have what I call a "personal foundation" upon which we choose to build our lives. It is a culmination of the results of our thoughts --which create our feelings, our fears, and our actions. For example, if our thought is that we can achieve a dream, our feelings and actions align themselves to that thought. Our attitude is positive and open. We take action based upon our belief that there are endless opportunities and roads that will lead us to where we want to go. We might take risks and stretch outside of our comfort zone, practice developing skills, investigate possible paths, or seek advice from a mentor. If our thought is that a dream is simply not possible, our feelings and actions would align with that thought. Our fear of failing might dominate our thoughts. If so, we would not practice new behaviors or building new skills. We would not seek a mentor. Our action would be to accept our current state, stay where we are, and do what we have always done before.

Our personal foundation is really the thoughts, beliefs, and behaviors that we build our life upon. It is our way of thinking and the real world outcomes of those thoughts. It is how we choose to show up in the world, what we tell ourselves, and how we interact with others. We can choose to show up as empowered and responsible for our own destiny or we can chose to show up as powerless, as a victim of whatever life throws our way. You might be thinking that no one would choose to be powerless. Yet, when we do not consciously choose to be accountable for our thoughts, feelings, and choices, we are choosing to give up the individual power we each have over our lives. In effect, we are choosing to be powerless. The more solid we are in our foundation, the more solid we are in our ability to create the lives of our dreams. As we go forward, I will share with you all of the tools you need to build a solid personal foundation. First let's talk about each of the five components of your personal foundation.

Five Components of Our Personal Foundation

1. Thoughts
2. Emotions
3. Fears
4. Actions
5. Results

Anything is possible for you.

Thoughts

We often underestimate the sheer power of our thoughts. Our thoughts are the most powerful tool we have. Our thoughts create, attract, or control every aspect of our lives. We are what we think. Our thoughts create every facet of what we believe and how we interact in the world. Our thoughts create our entire belief system. They determine our values. They control whether our self-talk is positive or negative. They control every action, inaction, or reaction we have because everything we do or experience in life stems from thought. We decide to act based upon what we think and our thoughts are the motivation behind our every emotion and action.

We learn from a young age to process all of our experiences through a mechanism called "filtering". Filtering is the way in which we perceive incoming information. Filtering is our way of sorting input that makes sense to us based upon our current knowledge, belief system, and feelings about ourselves. When we run information through our mental filter, we are essentially assimilating information in alignment with what we believe to be true at any given moment. For example, if someone says to me, "Wow, that is an interesting shirt", my filtering system may interpret that statement as a compliment, as a criticism, or simply as a statement of fact with no underlying meaning depending on how I perceive the situation, how I personally feel about myself, and even how I feel about the shirt. How I interpret that comment or incoming information depends upon my thought process or my filtering process.

Experts think that each one of us has approximately 60,000 thoughts per day. Whether we notice it or not, we expend a huge amount of energy thinking our thoughts. Imagine what would happen if we each choose to harness the power of those thoughts in a positive and empowering way. Imagine what our lives could become if we were able to rid ourselves of negative self-talk, fear, worry, and stress.

Emotions

Our emotions are very complex, but they always come about as a result of our thoughts. When we choose a thought and then attach emotion to that thought, we create a belief. Because we have the power to choose our thoughts, we also have the power to choose our emotions and our beliefs. Yes, that is often a challenging concept to digest, but it is true. Many people feel that we do not have any control over our emotions, that feelings are reactions to outside stimuli. Feelings are reactions, but what we feel is dependent upon our mental state and our ability to choose thoughts that are in alignment with our true self. When I say "true self", I am referring to the person that each of us was born to be. Our true self is the happy, curious, gifted person that we truly are inside without the clutter of self-doubt and fear.

Feelings are transient. They come and go and change depending upon our ability to choose self-actualizing thoughts. As we increase self-trust, we begin to rely more upon thoughts from our inner wisdom rather than from outside opinions. When we increase self-trust, we begin to shift our feelings. Feelings don't just happen to us; we create them based upon our level of fear and our level of self-trust. The more we are able to trust ourselves and our intuition, the less reactive we become in challenging situations. Our emotions do not dictate our reactions when we choose to take full responsibility for our lives and stand by our commitments and values. When we consciously choose to live by our commitments, our emotions follow. We become proactive instead of reactive.

> *Feelings don't just happen to us; we create them based upon our level of fear and our level of self-trust. The more we are able to trust ourselves and our intuition, the less reactive we become in challenging situations.*

I would never ask you to deny any feeling that you have. Your feelings are your feelings and it is important to acknowledge them, whatever they are in any given moment. There are no bad or wrong feelings. In fact, acknowledging what you are feeling is critically important to creating the life you want because your feelings can serve as a navigator. Emotions and feelings are an inner guide and a tool that we can use to gain awareness. Emotions offer us great knowledge and insight into ourselves. They tell us when we are on the path to true fulfillment and they tell us when it is time to make adjustments in our course. Our emotions tell us where we are in our growth process; they reveal opportunities to take responsibility for our choices; and they are a call to action. I will talk more about this later.

I am also going to make a distinction between empowering emotions and self-defeating emotions. To me, empowering or positive emotions bring us a feeling of personal empowerment and fulfillment. Empowerment does not mean gaining power over another person. Empowerment means having the feeling of being able to create our best life from the inside out. Fulfilling and empowering feelings are the emotions such as curiosity, self-love, joy, and excitement. They are the feelings that we are meant to feel when we are our true self and are on the road to living our best life. On the other hand, self-defeating or negative emotions are emotions that leave us stuck feeling powerless. They cut us off from our possibilities and they negatively impact our center, our natural state of being, and our peace of mind. The overall goal, when we feel any negative emotions, is to be able to move through the feelings not get stuck in them. Acknowledge the feelings, take time to process them, and then choose to align your actions with your commitments. We must feel our emotions, but then proactively choose to stand by our commitments and our personal truth. I believe the purpose of any negative or disempowering emotion is to serve as a wake up call that we are not living up to the highest possible expression of our true selves. Nor are we being fully responsible for our life and our choices.

Fears

When we are children, we learn not to touch a hot stove. We are either told that we will experience pain or we experience the pain of a burn first hand. We learn that fear tells us when danger is close. Fear helps us avoid pain. It is a safety mechanism. The same mechanism that keeps us safe as a child, that teaches us not to touch a hot stove, also teaches us to keep ourselves safe in other ways. We develop a voice in our head, a voice of warning that perceives impending pain. We learn that the voice protects us from harm and keeps us safe. Then, it seems that the line between true safety and perceived safety gets blurred. We know we have trusted that voice in the past and we begin to believe that everything it says is true.

The problem is that most of the time our "fear" is *false evidence appearing real,* a perception that we create with our thoughts in order to avoid pain. Most of the time, we are not in true danger. We are attempting to avoid perceived emotional danger: fear of rejection, fear of failure, fear of appearing foolish, fear of being alone, etc. Fear is simply a thought, a voice in our head, and a safety mechanism.

Fear is also the roadblock preventing us from living our best life. It is the roadblock that keeps us justifying our excuses, holding on to our self-limiting thoughts, and keeps us blaming others for the state of our lives. Fear can be very loud or subtle, but ultimately, it robs us of our peace of mind and our happiness. It shows up in our thoughts and behaviors in a variety of ways. Fear is truly the one and only roadblock stopping us from going where we want to go, doing what we want to do, and creating the life of our dreams.

> *I believe the purpose of any negative or disempowering emotion is to serve as a wake up call that we are not living up to the highest possible expression of our true selves. Nor are we being fully responsible for our life and our choices.*

We all have fears. No one is immune. Even people we might see as being profoundly successful have fears. We all want to feel a purpose, connect with others, feel valued in this world, and feel good about who we are. There are no exceptions. Many of us do not relate to the word "fear" because we associate it with weakness or being timid. We want to see ourselves as fearless, not fearful. I know I did not see my fear. I saw myself as a very strong, driven, fearless person. Yet, fear was playing a significant role in my inability to be true to myself when I interacted in the world. Fear kept me from being true to myself and my own needs, wants, and desires. Fear kept me living outside of my true self instead of embracing all of who I am.

For each of us, fear can show up in a variety of different ways. It can cause us to dwell on what is wrong in our lives instead of seeing what is right. It can keep us stuck in inaction. It can keep us stuck trying to prove that we are "right" so that our ego will feel better, instead of giving ourselves permission to follow the inner wisdom of our hearts. It can keep us on the hamster wheel of life trying to live up to a standard that we believe we should be able to achieve. Fear can cause us to feel stressed, unfulfilled, and emotionally and physically drained.

Pay attention to what your life and your emotions are saying to you. Based on my personal experience and my experience with clients, I believe that anytime we feel stressed, frustrated, frazzled, or any other negative emotion, fear is somehow involved. There are great gifts in the moments of fear if we choose to see them. Noticing fear is an opportunity for awareness and ultimately change. Look for the red flags in your life.

Fear is also…

Fear of being an outcast, fear of intimacy, fear of being vulnerable

Fear of aging or dying

Feeling defensive, reactive, or keeping your guard up at all times

Being self-righteous or holding a grudge

Fear of failing, succeeding, rejection, or not being worthy

Feeling bored, unfulfilled with life, or just going through the motions

Over-apologizing or inability to apologize

Inability to accept responsibility for your role in your life challenges

Taking things personally or assuming you know what the other person is thinking

Negative self-talk or self-blame

Living in denial or pretending you are ok when you are not

Avoiding facing a tough conversation

Inaction, paralysis, or procrastination that impedes fulfilling responsibilities

Lying, omitting the truth, or inability to speak honesty

Feeling afraid to set boundaries or tell others what you want

Complaining, whining, worrying

Waiting for someone else to fix it for you or hoping the problem will just go away

Wanting others to see you as perfect and worrying what others think

Judging, controlling, or forcing your opinions upon others

Staying angry about a situation and not asking for what you want

Blaming someone else for everything that is wrong in your life

Abusing drugs, alcohol, food, or any substance

Spending, gambling, or exercising in excess

Comparing yourself to others or seeking approval in order to feel secure or content

Putting people down, being overly critical, or name calling

Shutting down, checking out emotionally, living in loneliness, or isolating yourself

People pleasing at the expense of your own needs

Gossiping, thriving on drama, or exaggerating the truth

Forecasting negative outcomes

Being aggressive instead of assertive, raging with anger

Feeling victimized, wronged, or powerless
Feeling guilty or focusing on what you should have done
Focusing on fault, blame, or jealousy
Building evidence to prove you are right or seeing only your side of the story
Resisting the truth or reality of any situation

True empowerment does not come from hiding our fears, but from learning to uncover, embrace, and master them. If we can see fear as a call to action, we can begin to master fear and even use it to propel us forward. No matter where we are in our life journey, we must make the choice to act on our commitments and reach for our dreams, despite our feelings of fear. When we decide to begin to master our fear, life changes in ways we could never have imagined.

> *True empowerment does not come from hiding our fears, but from learning to uncover, embrace, and master them. If we can see fear as a call to action, we can begin to master fear and even use it to propel us forward. No matter where we are in our life journey, we must make the choice to act on our commitments and reach for our dreams, despite our feelings of fear.*

Actions

Our actions are our behaviors, our habits, our words, and our deeds. As with thoughts and emotions, we always have a choice in how we choose to act. Every action or inaction is our choice. We can choose to stay where we are or we can choose to move forward. We can choose to share the best of our true selves with others or we can choose to act with malice. We can choose to act on our emotions or we can choose to act on our commitments. There is always a choice in what action we take.

What stops us from taking action in an empowering way? We get into the groove and go with the flow as if we were floating down a river with no oars. We get comfortable with the familiar. Yet, there are times when we want to go with the flow and there are times we want to grab a branch and create a rudder. We are creatures of habit and all of our habits are learned behaviors. Habits are also actions that begin with thoughts. They are actions that are repeated with consistency. All habits are first learned and then become automatic responses or behaviors. Positive habits are fine, as long as they empower us. Habits can create reliability and organization. Yet, habits become counterproductive when they become ruts and we feel like we are stuck spinning our wheels, going no where in our lives.

What would cause us to continue a habit even though it is stopping us from creating the life that we want? I believe that fear and stepping into the unfamiliar are the primary roadblocks to achieving our goals. Yet, sometimes we just are not aware that it is *fear* motivating our actions. We fall back into our old ways because our old patterns seem easier, require less effort, and they are familiar. We must remember two things:

1) ANY action repeated with consistency becomes habit.

2) The rewards of taking a step forward are far greater than the most justified reason for standing still.

Deciding to master fear or expand your life requires practicing new thoughts and behaviors. Just as our old habits were learned, we can choose to practice learning new behaviors and develop behaviors that propel us forward. Having the awareness of what thoughts, emotions, and behaviors are holding you back is the first step. The next step is committing to do something differently and then following through with action. We may or may not be able to change our old habits in an instant, but we can choose to practice taking action that moves us in a new direction. If we truly desire lasting change, we must be willing to practice thinking new thoughts and choosing new behaviors.

Behaviors develop primarily for two reasons: our actions seem to get us our desired results or we just do not have the knowledge or skills to act differently. We work with the knowledge and skills we have. My daughter had her share of tantrums when she was young. She desired two results: she wanted attention and she wanted to get her way. She was our third child in five years and tantrums seemed to get her the results she was seeking. Tantrums brought her attention and they got her what she wanted because I was often too tired to hold my position. She did what worked and she did what she knew how to do. For a while, tantrums became an automatic response for her. At some point, as a parent, I decided that her behavior was no longer going to get her what she wanted. I began to ignore her when she had inappropriate outbursts. She soon figured out that tantrums no longer got her what she wanted and her behaviors changed. As she matured, she learned how to achieve her goals by developing more effective skills. We can all do that, no matter what age we are or what our current behaviors are.

Results

Every minute of every day, we are creating results whether we realize it or not. I once heard the definition for "insanity" is doing the same thing over and over again and expecting to get a different result. I agree. The only way to get something different is to do something different. It is cause and effect. If you want a new result, think a new thought and take a new action.

If we attempt to do something new and we do not achieve our desired result, our fear wants to tell us that we have failed or even worse, we see ourselves as a failure. The truth is there are great lessons in results. Results are teachers. Results teach us whether our thoughts, feelings, and actions are getting us what we want. They show us whether we are on the right track or we need to adjust our course. As we move through the journey of life, our results are one more tool that we can use to guide us to living our best life. Results are simply outcomes of decisions and actions.

Personal Foundation Questions

Our personal foundation is built upon our thoughts, emotions, fears, actions, and results. As we have talked about, everything that we are currently experiencing in our lives today has come about as a result of our thoughts. Our thoughts create our emotions and our thoughts create our fears. When we attach emotion to our thoughts, they become beliefs and we tend to take action based upon our beliefs. Actions create habits and actions create results. The culmination of it all creates the experiences of our daily lives. So essentially, everything we know to be true at this very moment, we have created through our personal foundation.

The most extraordinary aspect of our personal foundation is that we can change our reality and our experiences simply by changing our thoughts. I can tell you with 100% certainty that this is true. I have experienced it first hand and I have witnessed countless clients change their lives by changing their thoughts. Since everything we know, believe, and feel stems from thoughts, we have the power within us to change any or every aspect of our life. Thoughts do not change circumstances, but they do change our ability to mentally access our possibilities.

Remember that each of our personal foundations is as unique as we are. Our own thoughts, feelings, fears, and actions influence how we apply the Life Laws to our individual circumstances. As you integrate each of the Life Laws into your daily life, please use the following questions as a guide to understanding where you are in your journey and what is holding you back.

Thoughts:

What are the thoughts you are thinking about a particular situation?

Are your thoughts in alignment with self-trust or fear?

If you had complete self-trust, what would your thoughts be?

What information can you gain that would give you more clarity?

Emotions:

What feelings come up as a result of your thoughts?

Would you classify them as self-empowering or self-defeating?

What feelings would be empowering?

What would have to happen for you to be able to feel that way?

Fears:

What underlying fears might be driving your thoughts?

What internal roadblocks to your happiness do you sense?

What external roadblocks to do you perceive?

How might these perceived external roadblocks be related to fear?

Actions:

What is your responsibility in this situation?

What are you personally committed to in this situation?

What is your overall goal?

What actions can you take that are in alignment with your commitments and goals?

Results:

What results are you getting?

What results do you want?

What can you choose to do differently to increase the likelihood of getting the results you desire?

Chapter 2

Take Action.
Life Expands Through Risk.

"Come to the edge, Life said. They said, We are afraid.
Come to the edge, Life said. They came.
It pushed Them...
And they flew." —Apollinaire

What do you really, really want in your life? What are you willing to do *today* to make that happen? Many of us say that we want to live our best life. We want to make changes, but we don't know where to begin, what to do, or how to change our circumstances. Yet, it is not our circumstances that create our lives; it is our thoughts, actions, and responses to those circumstances that determine the quality of our lives. If we are unhappy with any circumstance in our life, how do we respond? Do we just believe that we have no choice? Do we sit and fret about all of the inequities in the world? Do we let fear control our thinking and our actions? Or do we set out to make changes? I have found that fear and love are the two primary driving forces that motivate action or inaction. Fear fosters emotional reactivity, defensiveness, and paralysis. Love motivates us to be proactive, self-trusting, and responsible for creating our best life. We have a choice to live in our fears or master them.

We have a choice to learn to trust ourselves and take action or stay stuck where we are.

The Law of Action

The Law of Action states that we only gain true understanding of our possibilities in life when we decide to take action, despite any fears or roadblocks. We gain skill, trust, and wisdom when we choose to take action and choose to move toward our dreams. We have no way of knowing the true depths of our knowledge, our gifts, or capabilities unless we decide to take action in our lives. We have no way of knowing the extent of our potential until we put effort into learning about ourselves. Our lives expand when we take action and our lives remain stagnant with inaction. We can have all of the knowledge in the world, but is meaningless until it is applied. We can have the most creative and inspiring dream, but it is merely a dream until we decide to act on our idea. We can be surrounded by the most brilliant mentors, but we stand motionless until we are open to learning from them. We may wish for respect, but until we are willing to set boundaries and command respect, our lives will not change. We may desire peace of mind, but until we take action to create peace, we will not initiate change. Only action is action.

Each time we take action, we learn more about ourselves and our capabilities. We grow as human beings. It is like turning a light on in a dark room. The light shines and reveals what is inside. As the poem by Apollinaire at the beginning of this chapter infers, when we decide to take action in spite of roadblocks or fears, we learn that we can reach beyond our current perceived limitations. Action brings our potential to life. It unveils aspects of our true self that we may not have been aware of. Think about it, until we apply effort, we have no way of knowing what we are capable of achieving and we have no way of knowing how blissful life can feel when we attempt to "fly".

I talked with a client recently who readily acknowledged that she had many fears. She was afraid to go too far away from home; she was afraid to drive long distances alone; and she was afraid of heights. She knew that her fears were holding her back in every aspect of her life and she decided to start facing them. She decided to drive twelve hours from home to visit friends who lived in the mountains. While there, she climbed a mountain path to the top of a ridge and looked down over the gorgeous countryside, looking at the emerald green tree tops, the textured rocks and boulders, and the clear blue pools of water. She had never seen such beauty before. It was a significant turning point in her life, not only because she had witnessed such a beautiful sight, but because she learned that she was capable of so much more than she had ever thought possible. She gained knowledge about her own inner gifts and strengths. She had more self-pride and self-confidence than she ever had before. She learned that only those of us who take action, break free of fear, and make the climb, can enjoy the riches of the summit. As I listened to her describe the experience, I got goose bumps because I knew she was on the cusp of creating her best life.

Expecting others to act for us does not support our growth because it is only from our own action that we learn we can rise above our fears and depend on ourselves. As a parent, I am very cognizant of this concept with my children. It is my nature to want to see my children happy, to want to spare them from hurt, and to want to help them when they face a challenge. Yet, I know in my heart that if I rescue them from every challenge and every potential hurt, they will not learn the self-reliance skills that they need in order to live a fulfilling life. I can actually hurt them in the long run if I continuously fix their problems for them. I must be willing to be a guide and a loving supporter as *they* work through their challenges. Only when they learn that they can handle any challenge or fear that they face, will they have true freedom in life. It is what we all strive for. The only time we ever really need courage is when we face fear. Each of us grows stronger when we can be courageous to act on our commitments despite our fear.

Action is practicing mastering new skills, living each day on purpose with purpose, and celebrating every step forward. Action is enjoying the journey of life. Taking action does not necessarily mean going skydiving or climbing Mount Everest. Although, if that is your goal, go for it! Taking action means deciding to start doing something differently today. It is making a commitment to practice new thoughts and behaviors. It might be something as simple as changing your attitude about a specific situation or something as complex as changing your career, but action is movement. It is not just reading about using these concepts; it is applying them to your life, developing new skills, and working toward mastery. Trust me when I say that people who have successful, passionate lives do not have fewer challenges than less successful people; they just know how to take action to move forward. They have an attitude of forging on no matter what obstacles they face. They are resilient and continually take action to move toward their goals.

There is a difference between acting and reacting. When we choose to take action based upon our commitments, we practice and build habits that move us forward. If we practice a thought or behavior with consistency, it will become an automatic response and we will react in accordance. For example, a golfer that practices using proper form to develop her golf swing will develop automatic skills when she plays in a tournament. When a fireman trains through practicing during mock drills, he will react based upon his training during a fire. Reactions become automatic responses as a result of practice. In the same way reactions can be beneficial, reactions can also be destructive if our habits are destructive. If our reactions are impulsive and based upon perceptions and emotions, instead of fact or training, they can keep us stuck in our negative patterns. We tend to repeat behaviors that are familiar and that are within our comfort zone. If we are going to create the life we really want, we must be vigilant and notice how we are acting and reacting. We must decide to act in empowering ways. Remember our actions or responses are based upon our own thoughts, *not the words or deeds of anyone else*. If your reaction is to become defensive when your boss asks you a question, what beliefs or patterns keep *you* reacting that way? If someone yells at you, do you react by yelling back or are you able to remain calm? Do you react differently with different people?

The Comfort Zone

Our comfort zone is any thought, feeling, or action that we have essentially become comfortable in doing. It is unique to each one of us. What may feel uncomfortable to one person may feel comfortable to someone else. For example, some of us may have a comfort zone that includes public speaking. We might feel very comfortable standing in front of a group of people and conveying information. Others of us might feel uneasy speaking to a group, but feel at ease making conversation with people one on one. Others, still, might be much more comfortable with books or computers than with any people.

Our comfort zone is a description of what is safe, comfortable, and familiar to each of us. It can include empowering behaviors that utilize our strengths and skills or behaviors that keep us stuck doing what we have always done before. Your comfort zone could be seeing the negative side of every situation or spending your time dreaming instead of doing. You could be comfortable responding in anger, thriving on drama, or avoiding confrontation. The comfort zone is where we feel safe in our patterns and behaviors, whether or not those behaviors are positive or negative. It is where we are safe from facing our fear of doing things differently.

People say they want growth, change, or something different, but making changes feels uncomfortable. When we choose to live inside our comfort zone knowing we want more for ourselves, we are choosing to let fear run our lives. In essence, the comfort zone is the greatest enemy of possibility, creativity, and human potential because living within our comfort zone prohibits us from stretching, growing and striving to reach our potential.

What keeps us inside our comfort zone? Sometimes we don't know what to do and we wait for someone to show us the way. Some of us want a guarantee of positive results before we make a move. Sometimes we are just willing to settle for the way things are, thinking that this is as good as it gets or this is all we deserve. Sometimes we make excuses about time, money, or responsibilities. We blame our circumstances or other people for holding us back. There are many reasons we don't move forward. You might not want to look foolish or incompetent, so you procrastinate. Maybe you are taking action, but you are taking action based in fearful way, trying to avoid the prospect of feeling pain or emotional discomfort. Maybe you are feeling guilty because you think you should be grateful for what you do have.

I believe the bottom line is we all get stuck in our habits and ruts because we don't want to leave our comfort zone. We don't want to leave our comfort zone because stepping out of it is uncomfortable and unfamiliar. Our fear leaves us immobilized. It is easier to interact with people the way we have always done and stay in our current routines, than to do something completely outside of our norm. Unfortunately, people stay in bad relationships, unrewarding jobs, push themselves to their limits, sacrifice their health and happiness, and suffer humiliation because breaking out of old habits and patterns is just too scary. What is your comfort zone costing you? We all have our reasons for staying safe. Venturing into the unknown can leave you feeling vulnerable and open to rejection or failure.

Turning Vulnerability into Invincibility

Breaking free of our comfort zone and our fear requires us to become vulnerable because stepping out of our comfort zone is stepping into the unknown. We might feel unsure, unprotected, and exposed to feeling pain. For many people, "vulnerability" sounds like a bad word. Like the word "fear", it implies weakness. Being vulnerable means feeling exposed or susceptible to injury, attack, or criticism. I know you are thinking, based on that definition, who would want to be vulnerable? Yet, we overcome any insecurity we may have by welcoming vulnerability and being open to taking risks.

A risk is any thought or action that is out of the norm for you. When you step out of your comfort zone, you are taking a risk by venturing into the unknown. It is through risking that we learn that we can not only survive, but thrive in the face of fear. Vulnerability really is the key to invincibility. If we can step outside of our comfort zone and embrace those moments of vulnerability, we learn that we can handle anything that comes our way. We learn that we grow when we face our fear. We learn that we can bounce back from anything. Imagine being able to expand your life by stepping out of your comfort zone knowing with 100% certainty and self-trust that you can handle any result. That is invincibility and it is possible for any one of us. Being emotionally invincible, it does not mean that we keep our armor on. It means that we have enough self-trust to know that we can recover from any trial, tribulation, loss or challenge that we face. So how does vulnerability lead to invincibility in life? Here is an example:

Elizabeth had experienced the loss of a relationship. The pain she felt colored her thinking and her approach to meeting new people. She went on a string of blind dates, but only seemed to meet "jerks". She felt no connection with any of the men she was dating and the sting of her past relationship was still vivid. She had almost lost all hope when she and I began our coaching relationship. She discovered in our sessions that she fully anticipated experiencing the pain and loss of her past again.

Elizabeth believed that the past would repeat itself and she would end up feeling hurt. Unknowingly, she built up emotional walls to keep herself safe. She did not connect with any of the men she dated because she was not willing to be her authentic self when she went out on dates. She showed up as someone who was not willing to get hurt, someone who kept her guard up. Her body language was closed and her verbal language was curt. She built evidence against each suitor and judged their every word. She unconsciously wanted to be in a position of power instead of feeling vulnerable. She could not connect on a human level while engaged in a power struggle.

Elizabeth decided to take action in slow, but consistent steps. She decided that she would share at least one personal aspect of herself on each date and she decided to see the person on the other side of the table as a human being instead of a potential destroyer of her heart. She also decided that each time she felt judgmental, she would ask more questions instead of making assumptions. When Elizabeth was willing to open her heart to love, even with the possibility of loss, she was able to connect and find love.

If we were to become invincible in our daily lives, what qualities would we have? We would have trust in our ability to handle any challenge that comes our way. We would have the ability to share our true self with our friends, loved ones, and co-workers without fear of judgment or pain. We would honor our own needs as well as respect the needs of others. We would have self-confidence and see the limitless possibilities available to us. Most of all, we would have control over our fears and seek to expand our comfort zone on a consistent basis. Each time we took a risk and stepped out of our comfort zone, our fear would still show up, but we would have mastery over it. We would acknowledge it and take action anyway. In order to strive for invincibility, we must be willing to take risks and to feel uncomfortable. Vulnerability is strength. We must be willing to be vulnerable and step out of our comfort zone.

> *If we can step outside of our comfort zone and embrace those moments of vulnerability, we learn that we can handle anything that comes our way. What is staying in your comfort zone costing you?*

Building Confidence

The only true way to master fear and expand your comfort zone is through action and risk. The only true way to build confidence is through action and risk. Many of us believe that having more confidence is the key to breaking free of fear. I have heard my clients say that if they had more confidence, they could handle facing challenging conversations; if they had more confidence, they could find love; if they had more confidence, they could travel more, open a business, or ask for a raise. This is the great fallacy about self-confidence. It is not something we have or don't have. Self-confidence is something we build by taking steps or risks outside of our comfort zone and facing our fear. Self-confidence is like a muscle that grows with exercise and practice. To get more confidence in any area, we must choose to move beyond the safe, familiar, and comfortable. The more we take risks, the more our confidence grows. The more we take risks, the more we learn to trust that we can handle any result, regardless of any doubts or fears lurking around in our minds.

Think of a child who is learning to walk. The child practices pulling himself up by leaning on a chair or couch. Once he masters standing, he might venture a little farther out of his comfort zone by sliding his foot forward. If he gets off balance and falls, he makes his way back to the chair and starts again. It may take some time, but he keeps trying. Eventually, he is putting one foot in front of the other and starts to walk. His comfort zone has now expanded and he trusts himself. He practices. He pushes himself. He starts to walk and then to run.

Taking action outside of your comfort zone feels uncomfortable and risky, but with each step forward, the boundaries of your comfort zone expand. Your knowledge expands and your confidence expands. The only way to overcome your fear of anything is to go out and face it, even if it is by taking tiny steps and even when it feels uncomfortable. Every step forward has value and every step counts as taking a risk. Every step forward builds your confidence.

Say you are watching the young child again, reaching his foot out to take a first step. He takes a step, he wobbles, and then he falls. What would you do as someone who is watching him? Would you humiliate him for not succeeding? Of course not. You would celebrate his willingness to try and encourage him to try again. He has, in fact, made progress even though he fell. He has learned more about balance and coordination as he took that step. Somehow as we grow up, we get it in our heads that trying and falling is failure. We think that we are going to be laughed at and feel humiliated. It is our perception. If someone does laugh at us, what is the worst thing that could happen? I cannot think of anything worse than giving up on myself and my dreams. I can live with laughter, but I cannot live with giving up.

It is our responsibility to stay on course and strive to live our best life. It is our responsibility to find the courage to *practice* the skills we want to master. As you step out of your comfort zone, focus on what you are doing and what you will gain, not how you are feeling, because you will feel uncomfortable. Stepping forward is what propels us to reaching our possibilities. Every time we step out of our comfort zone by taking a risk, we learn to trust ourselves more in that particular area. As we get more experience and gain competence, our confidence grows. Building trust in our abilities builds our self-confidence. Building trust in ourselves builds our self-esteem. We learn that we can count on ourselves. We learn that setbacks are part of the process. We learn that we can shake them off and keep trying.

> *The only way to build confidence is by taking risks and stepping outside of your comfort zone. Your confidence grows as your competence grows. As you take risks, focus on the actions you are taking, not how you are feeling. Taking a risk will feel uncomfortable, but it is a sign of growth.*

We are energy. Our lives are energy. When we give energy direction, the energy has purpose. When it is left with no direction, it takes on random form and can even become destructive. Everyday we choose how we expend our energy: in the same direction or a new direction, in an empowering way or a disempowering way. The way you live your life is your choice. There are situations that are out of your control, but you have absolute control over YOU. You choose how you respond to any event, situation, or person. You choose to be resistant or you choose to be open to change. You choose to move forward or stay stuck in your emotions. Action is being fully accountable for every aspect of your life and it is the key to change. The moment that you truly embrace the truth, that your life is controlled by you on every level of your being, your life will begin to change in ways you never could have imagined.

No Victims Here

Action is taking full and complete responsibility for your life, pushing beyond your current comfort zone, and embracing new experiences. Action also requires us to embrace the idea that we are not victims of our circumstances. We may not be able to control every aspect of our circumstances, but we can control our thinking, actions, and responses. Action requires us to see clearly that making changes is completely up to us. No one is coming to swoop in and create the life of our dreams for us. No one is coming to our rescue. We must decide to take action to create our best life and get out of our own way.

My client, Jerry, once said to me, "After everything that they have done to me, I deserve to feel the way I do." Jerry was angry, disappointed, hurt, and felt that he was treated unfairly. We probably have all experienced this feeling at some point in our lives. Yet, we need to get over the idea that life will always seem fair. There are many forces at work that we may never fully comprehend, but we must accept the reality of *what is* not what we think it is supposed to be. The rest of the world does not always do what we want them to do and things don't always go our way. That is the reality of life.

Jerry's feelings may or may not have been valid, but his language told me that he was stuck in them anyway, stuck in the disappointment, stuck in the resentment, and stuck feeling like a victim. Getting stuck in our negative emotions keeps us victimizing ourselves because our anger or resentment does not change the issue or the outcome. We become our own roadblock by choosing to stay where we are. When Jerry chooses to stay in those feelings long term, he is only robbing himself of living his best life. He is robbing himself of his own energy and happiness. Again, all negative or self-defeating emotions are a call to action to continue to move forward, regardless of the circumstance.

Why It Happened Does Not Change Anything

Many of us tend to ponder the "why" in our lives. Why did this happen to me? Why can't I get my dream job? Why did I have to grow up the way I did? Why did my marriage turn out this way? Why can't I find love? Why am I so tired? The keys to your happiness do not lie in understanding the "why". The "why" keeps us reviewing the negative circumstances over and over in our mind. It blocks us from accepting the truth of where we are and from seeing any good in our situation. Please trust me when I say to you that everything that happens in our lives can push us toward our greatness if we are open.

Life lessons come to us in ways we do not always understand. Misfortune happens to good people. Yet, in every event, without exception, there is an opportunity to learn, to grow, or to become stronger. Life lessons come to us to show us that everything we need to live our best life, our authentic life, is within us. Life lessons are meant to teach us something. If we can see that every event is put before us in order to propel us forward, we can move into action instead of getting stuck. We must listen to what our life is telling us and showing us.

We must move from "why" to "how". How am I going to move through my disempowering feelings and find my center, my joy, my inner wisdom? How can I see this challenge as an opportunity? How can I turn this situation around and gain knowledge from it? How am I going to take steps forward to create the life I want? How am I going to take responsibility for my life and take action in a positive way?

Decide What You Want

What do you want to change or enhance as you take your life journey? Think of a goal or something that you always wanted to try, but never did. Have you accomplished great things, but still feel unfulfilled? What are you tolerating that you no longer want to tolerate? Are you surviving instead of thriving? In order to take action, you must have an idea of what you want or where you want to go. The more clarity you have on what you want, the more clearly you will see opportunities as they arise. Your journey may take twists and turns. It may lead you to possibilities that you have never imagined. It is important to decide on a target and then take action steps to move toward your goal.

One of my clients had a favorite saying, "How do you eat an elephant? One bite at a time." I love this saying because sometimes our goals feel overwhelming and we have no clue where to begin, so we must take it one step at a time. The most important step is deciding to take action. Start where you are and move forward, one step at a time. It is not possible to reach your goals while standing still and avoiding action. As hockey star, Wayne Gretzky once said, "You miss 100% of the shots you don't take." What do *you* want for your life?

Do you want to:

Find love…Change careers…Enhance your relationships…Learn to say no…Learn to say yes…Change old habits…Let go of suffering…Communicate more effectively…Trust yourself… Find peace of mind… Forge your own path… Break free of limitations… Be more decisive… Move somewhere new… Ask for a promotion… Feel passion for life… Stop talking and start doing… Follow a dream… Inspire others… Be more positive and open… Be a more connected parent, spouse, friend… Build confidence… Become self employed… Give up worrying…Give up trying to be perfect… Perform in front of an audience…Write a book… Motivate your team… Be proactive, not reactive… Land your dream job… Feel centered and happy…Get physically fit…Explore something new…Take a class…Live full out...Trust your instincts... Laugh, have more fun, and feel joy... Achieve sales goals...Get unblocked... Access your creativity... Become a leader...Master fear... Choose your own path... Stop making everyone else's needs more important than your own... Be the star in your life... Get off the hamster wheel... Let go of your excuses... Express your feelings...Be yourself...Really Live!

I can hear some of you now. "Yes, I would like to make changes in my life, but I can't. I don't have enough time. I don't have enough money. I don't have enough experience or education. With all of my responsibilities, I barely make it through the day right now. I have so many bills. I don't have time to relax or exercise. My spouse is not supportive. I can't take on one more thing! You don't understand. My situation is different..." These are all justifications for staying stuck. Your situation is not necessarily different. The topics and circumstances may be different, but the net result is the same. You choose to be exactly where you are. You are where you are because of the thoughts that you think and the actions that you take or do not take.

> *True empowerment does not come from hiding our fears, but from learning to uncover, embrace, and master them. Let your fear alert you that it is time to make a change and take steps forward.*

Fear and Action

Fear is really the absence of trust in ourselves. When we truly trust ourselves fully and completely in any area of our life, fear is no longer the master. Fear is mastered. The first step toward the mastery of fear is identifying where fear plays a role in your life. If you are like me, fear may show up in subtle ways, but I promise you it is there. Everyone has fear on some level. If you think you don't, then maybe it is time to stretch beyond your comfort zone and take a risk.

Fear pops up each and every time we step outside of our comfort zone. When we master our fear, we feel the fear and act on our commitments anyway. You may be scared and your heart might race, but the feeling of fear is just a messenger alerting you that you are taking a risk.

True empowerment does not come from hiding our fears, but from learning to uncover, embrace, and master them. Let your fear alert you that it is time to make a change and take steps forward. When you can see fear as a call to action, you can begin to master fear and use it to propel you into living your life as your authentic self. We must make the choice to act on our commitments and reach for our dreams, despite our feelings of fear. When you decide to begin to master your fear, you begin to build more self-confidence and self-esteem.

The child who is learning to walk is relatively fearless. The goal of walking is bigger than the fear of failing, the fear of looking foolish, the fear of being judged, or the fear of rejection. I know this example sounds simplistic, but the fact is we must decide that our goal, any goal, anything we want to create in our lives, is bigger than our fear. Let your fear become a call to action to make a new choice instead of staying stuck where you are. Life offers choices between safety and risk each and every day. Taking action through risk is the key to freedom and part of risking is being willing to be vulnerable.

Remember only action is action. Don't just sit around and think about it, go out and do it! Take a step, any step. It will feel uncomfortable at first and it will require effort and commitment. Change your thoughts. Change your patterns. Get clear on what you want and then take action based on creating your highest probability for success. Start where you are with what you have. It is not necessary to have all of the answers and know what every step will be. The answers will come to you as you take action. Opportunities will present themselves. There is no perfect time or perfect circumstance. Create your life starting now. Take a step. Be willing to adjust your course and be willing to take a risk each and every day. Decide to dream, to let go of fear, to do things differently, and to live the life you have completely. Claim your life. Life is about living fully and action is the first step. Choose to take one risk each and every day.

Action Tools

As we go forward, I will share some specific tools that you can use to take action. I will also share some action exercises that will help you build more awareness and practice building your skills. I will refer to empowering and disempowering thoughts and behaviors. Disempowering thoughts and behaviors are those that are controlled by fear and self doubt. Empowering thoughts and behaviors are those that embrace possibility, personal responsibility, and fearlessness.

> *Disempowering thoughts are those controlled by fear and self doubt.*
> *Empowering thoughts embrace possibility, personal responsibility, and fearlessness.*

Create a Support Team

It is also critical to understand that we are not here to move through life alone. The life purpose for all of us is to connect with others in meaningful ways. For this reason, I encourage all of you to develop an "Action for Life Team". As you read this book, I encourage you to pay attention to the people that you interact with on a day to day basis. Do they support you and your growth? Who can you turn to when you need a mentor? Who in your life brings you down and in what areas of your life? If you are going to create the life you want, it is imperative to create a team that will support you in taking action steps to move beyond fear and disempowering behaviors. We all need support to fully access our potential.

Action for Life Exercise

How does fear impact your life?

What does it stop you from doing or achieving?

What do you really want for your life? Define what your ideal life looks like. What are five things that are present in your ideal life that are not present in your current life? How can you begin to build the life that you want?

What one area of your life do you want to work on most?

What one area of your life do you want to build more confidence? What risks are you willing to take to build your confidence muscle?

What are three things that you need to do in order to get closer to your desired outcome?

What action are you willing to take in the next 24 hours that is a risk or a step outside of your comfort zone?

What habits do you have that empower you?

How can you utilize your empowering habits to reach your goal?

What habits do you have that you know are disempowering you?

What is one habit you are willing to change in the next 24 hours? How will you be accountable?

What "why" are you willing to change to "how"?

Action for Life Team

Who in your life encourages you to take risks?

Who holds you back?

Who can provide sound advice or wisdom in the area you want to work on?

Who can you ask to help you be accountable?

Chapter Strategy

Turn immobility into action by stepping out of your comfort zone, risking, and building self-confidence. The only way to truly find out what you are capable of achieving is through action.

Chapter 2 Key Points

- Take Action. Life expands through risk.
- The Law of Action states that we can only discover the true depths of our talents, skills, and gifts by taking action. In order to become all that we are capable of, we must turn immobility into movement.
- Every current condition of your life has been created by you, initiated by your thoughts.
- Action is changing your thoughts feelings, attitudes, habits, and behaviors. It is taking full responsibility for your life, pushing out of your comfort zone, committing to practice, and moving forward.
- FEAR is often False Evidence Appearing Real
- Fear can be subtle or loud, but it is always a call to action.
- A risk is stepping outside of your comfort zone. A risk is thinking or doing something differently than you have done before.
- Vulnerability is the key to invincibility. When you risk and step outside of your comfort zone, you feel vulnerable. Yet, it is the act of risking that builds confidence, self-esteem, and momentum.
- Confidence is built only one way: by stepping out of your comfort zone.
- When you risk, focus on what you are doing, not how you are feeling, because you will feel uncomfortable. This discomfort is a sign of growth.

Chapter 3

You and Only You are Responsible for Your Life.

"You must take personal responsibility. You cannot change the circumstances, the seasons, or the wind, but you can change yourself."
--Jim Rohn

There is a secret that can change your life today, if you are willing to apply it. Imagine how your life could change if you only experienced agitation, frustration, irritation, or disappointment for a matter of moments? Imagine what could happen if the moment you noticed that you were upset, you could shift your thinking and move into more empowering emotions and actions. Imagine no more simmering in resentment or reviewing frustrating events over and over in your head. It is possible to be really centered and at peace without being passive or weak. The key is to get very clear about what you are truly responsible for, what is within the boundaries of your control, and what expectations of specific outcomes you are relying on to feel satisfied. Are you relying on yourself to create your life or are you giving that responsibility to someone else? Are you keeping your personal power or giving your power away?

The Law of Expectations

Expectations, by definition, are outcomes that we consider probable or certain; actions that we consider obligated or bound in duty; or assumptions that we believe are reasonable, due, or necessary. If we really examine this definition closely, "expectations" can have several very different meanings. Expectations can be the overall perspective that we use to look at the world around us, seeing the world as "for" us or "against" us. Expectations can also be a set of standards that we believe we "should" live by. They can be a self developed set of "rules" by which we measure ourselves and others. They can be spoken or unspoken. Expectations can be positive or negative, uplifting or defeating, assumptions or facts. The question becomes how are we using expectations in our life?

The Law of Expectations states that energy always follows thought and our experiences in life are a result of what we expect to experience. In our lives, we are limited only by our thoughts and beliefs about what is possible. What we ultimately experience in our life is a direct result of what we believe our limits or possibilities are. When we expect to see possibilities for ourselves, possibilities begin to appear. When we impose limits upon ourselves through our thoughts, the limits become our reality. Our perceptions of life are based upon what we expect to be true. We essentially create a reality based on what we think we deserve.

When expectations are empowering, they are anticipations or affirmations of a positive experience or state of being. To anticipate is to look forward to with pleasure without attachment to an outcome. Expectations of raising ourselves up to higher standards and higher goals are empowering expectations. To me, empowering expectations expand our thinking and our possibilities. They strip away our perceived limitations and doubts. For example, a child born into poverty who believes that the past does not equal the future may anticipate having opportunities for an abundant life. A coach may see raw talent in an athlete trying out for a team. A mother with a great family recipe and immense determination may plan to open a bakery. These expectations are a sign of belief and trust in ourselves or in someone else. They can push us out of our comfort zone and lead us to growth. If we can access the belief that the only limitations we truly have are those that are self imposed, we can begin to change our thinking. We can begin to anticipate a brighter, more fulfilling life. We can raise our anticipations to see a multitude of possibilities; yet, remain accepting of life as it unfolds.

I have talked at length about how confidence is developed by taking action and pushing beyond our current comfort zone. This works in conjunction with raising our anticipations of what is possible for each one of us. When we believe that achieving a dream is possible, there is a high probability for success. When we believe that we can do better, live by higher standards, and reach our goals, our beliefs set in motion a self-fulfilling prophecy. We do not measure ourselves by outside standards; we only focus on striving for our best life. The drive and determination comes from within and begins with our thoughts. We are realistic and know that challenges are inevitable. Yet, we see beyond any challenge and look to the bigger picture because our anticipations or empowering expectations expand our possibilities.

We all love stories about the power of the human spirit. In 1980, when the U.S. hockey team won in a stunning upset against the Soviets and then against Finland to take the gold medal, we were moved by the hearts of an underdog team believing against all odds that they could win. In 2003, when we heard about a high school cross-country runner with cerebral palsy, who never quit even though he fell flat several times during each race and crossed finish lines battered and bloody, we cheered for his spirit and determination. We have heard how people like Abraham Lincoln failed many times to get elected into the Congress and Senate prior to becoming the President of the United States. We also see ordinary people in our own communities do extraordinary things everyday, people who take risks to make a difference in someone else's life and people who overcome significant obstacles to live the life of their dreams. These people all believed in their possibilities, no matter their circumstances. What do you need to change in order to believe in your possibilities?

I believe that expectations are meant to manifest the calling of our higher self, our authentic, or our true self. They are meant to inspire us to strive for more and attract abundance to our lives. However, expectations can also be the catalyst for many disempowering emotions. It is critical to understand that expectations are empowering *only when* we are able to adhere to a few important guidelines.

Guidelines for Expectations:

- Expectations are meant to expand our thinking and our beliefs about what is possible in life.

- Expectations are empowering when we release ALL attachment to the outcome.

- Expectations are damaging or self-defeating when we use them in an attempt to control outcomes, situations, or other people.

When we do not adhere to these guidelines, expectations can become destructive to our overall well being. In this case, expectations lead us to disappointment, resentment, and reveal our lesser self. So, the real question becomes: **what are your expectations doing to you?** Are they creating inner turmoil or are they inspiring you to create your best life? Do they encourage you to be responsible for your life and your choices or do they make someone else responsible for your happiness? Do they have obligation attached or are they intentional choices?

> Expectations become destructive when we use them to attempt to control outcomes, situations, or other people.

Disempowering Expectations

Every time we have stringent expectations about how life *should* be, what our friends and loved ones *ought* to do, how our career *should* go, or any other such expectation, we are giving away our personal power and our ability to live our best life. When we expect, we are relying on someone or something to give us the outcome that we want. We are hoping for a result and if we don't get it, we get upset. When we expect and our expectations are not met, we are *always* disappointed. And that disappointment goes on to create resentment, anger, frustration, worry, mistrust, blame, or any other of a whole host of negative emotions. **In fact, every negative emotion we experience is attached to an unfulfilled expectation in some way.**

Reflect on a time when you were angry, annoyed, disappointed, or irritated. What were you expecting? What outcome were you attached to? Again, without exception, every negative emotion we experience is related to an unfulfilled expectation of someone or something. If you never have another expectation of a person, place, thing, situation, or yourself, you will never be annoyed or angry or frustrated again. If you do not get caught up in expecting a specific outcome, you will never be disappointed again. It is that simple. Pay attention to your emotions. They are the key to understanding where you are.

In daily life, harboring an expectation is harboring the belief that people should act a certain way, do certain things, or create a specific outcome. Expectations are essentially living in a world of "shoulds". Choosing to live in expectations is choosing to give up our own peace of mind. It is choosing to give up control over our life and our happiness. Mastering how we process our expectations is one of the keys to emotional freedom. Your negative emotions will reveal your expectations.

> *Without exception, every negative emotion we experience is related to an unfulfilled expectation of someone or something. If you never have another expectation of a person, place, thing, situation, or yourself, you will never be disappointed or angry or frustrated again. Pay attention to what your emotions are telling you.*

Here is an example: Let's say you are the kind of person that goes out of your way to remember people's birthdays and secretly, you expect all of your friends to remember you on your birthday. You decide not to ask them to remember you because then it would seem insincere. So, you keep your wishes to yourself. Your expectations are unspoken. Your friends do not know that you feel this way because you have never told them. You think that they *should* just know what you want. As your birthday arrives, you are filled with great expectations.

If they remember you on your birthday, you are happy. If they forget, you are disappointed. You might even be resentful or irritated because after all, you went out of your way to remember them. If they give you a present, you are thrilled. If they don't, you are bummed. The reality of the situation is that you have just given your ability to be happy to someone else. You are allowing your happiness to be determined by your friends, not by you. You are not relying on yourself to determine the state of your emotions. If they forget, what do your expectations get you? Disappointment. Do your expectations change the situation? No. Do your expectations change your friends? No. Does the fact that you are upset change the outcome? No.

Disempowering expectations do not change situations. They do not change other people. They do not change the outcomes. They only set us up for our own disappointment and they leave us stuck in our self-defeating emotions. They affect us and only us. Our disempowering expectations set *us* up because we are choosing to make someone else responsible for our feelings by attaching to a specific outcome. We are giving our power away and we pay the price through our negative emotions. Holding these expectations is like intentionally eating food that we know is contaminated. We are setting ourselves up to get sick. When we have the power to decide, why would we intentionally choose to give away our personal choice and personal power?

Expectations of Self

Even when we set expectations for ourselves, they are typically based upon what we think we *should* be able to do or how we think we *should* compare to the measuring stick of the outside world. Our expectations start in our minds. They start with our thoughts. I should be able to…A man should be able to…A mother should be able to… A friend should be able to…Someone with a business degree should be able to…Expectations of self are demands of ourselves to live up to a certain, often unrealistic, standard.

These expectations usually have a myopic point of view. In others words, we compare ourselves on specific attributes or activities without seeing the bigger picture, that we all are living in a unique set of circumstances. We set ourselves up for disappointment through our unrealistic expectations and when we fail to reach the unreachable bar we set for ourselves, we beat ourselves up. All of these expectations are disempowering!

> *Disempowering expectations set us up because we are attaching to a specific outcome. Notice when you use the word "should" in your life.*

We do not get to decide what other people do and they do not get to decide what we do. We all have free will and the ability to make our own choices. We do not get to control outcomes or people, outside of ourselves. Yet, we try over and over. That definition of insanity is coming to mind: insanity is repeating the same action and expecting a different result. It is almost as if we each create this imaginary rule book by which the rest of the world is supposed to live. We have specific mental rules for our children, rules for our co-workers, rules for our families, rules for our significant other, rules for our neighbors and friends, and rules for our employers. The problem is the rest of the world has not received a copy of *our* rule book. If you want people to know your rules, you better hand out your rule book! Attempting to get everyone else to live by our perceived rules is exhausting and futile. Again, we set ourselves up for disappointment and self-defeat when we attempt to control other people, situations, or outcomes.

People also try to live up to expectations that they feel are imposed upon them by others. My client, Andi, put herself through medical school and became a surgeon because that is what her parents wanted for her. She felt as if she was expected to get a certain level of education and live up to a certain standard. After she opened her medical practice, she was miserable. She decided that she was no longer going to live by the expectations of her parents and chose another career outside of medicine. When she broke free and followed her own dreams, she found success, happiness, and inner peace. When we allow other people's expectations to run our lives, we are not being true to ourselves or following our inner wisdom, the calling of our hearts. We cannot thrive living in disempowering expectations.

Yeah, But...*My* Expectations are Reasonable

I often hear the statement from clients, "yeah, but...my expectations are reasonable." "I feel like I have the right to feel this way. How can we realistically go through life with no expectations? What if someone gives their word, aren't we supposed to trust that they will keep it? What if we pay for a service, don't we have the right do expect to get what we paid for? How could anyone enter into marriage without expecting their partner to honor their vows? If we do not expect, aren't we really saying that we do not have any trust?" These questions are all valid.

We must realize that being a human being affords us the power of choice. It is not about reasonable or rights. What does "having the right" get you? Even if you have the right and the result is not what you want, does it change the outcome, the situation, or the other person? No! Having the right or not having the right is irrelevant because it does not change anything for *you* if your expectations are not met. When our expectations are unfulfilled, we get thrown into reaction mode. We experience the feelings of disappointment, resentment, and anger. The key is to release attachment to the outcome and to learn to look within ourselves for our own answers. It is up to us to decide how we will move forward.

It is not about trust either. When we enter into a marriage, it is our choice to do so. When we choose to trust, we give our trust because we want to, not because we are being forced. We all have free will. There is a difference between trusting and attaching to a specific outcome. There is also a difference between being responsible for our own life and expecting someone else to be responsible for our well being. We must be willing to see that all people make their own choices. In the grand scheme of life, we cannot control what other people do. We must learn how to be responsible for our lives, no matter what decisions other people make.

People enter into agreements with the best of intentions and then change their minds. People get married anticipating a long, happy life together, but marriages do end. People change their minds about careers, relationships, and commitments. People intend to keep their agreements, but they cannot control the economy, unforeseen circumstances, or the weather. Life happens; circumstances change; and they are not within our control. We do not get to control situations or people. Are we as human beings going to have expectations? Yes, without a doubt. However, we must focus on making choices that empower us or allow us to determine our own fate. Even if we make the decision to trust and we are let down, we are still responsible for working through our own feelings. We are still responsible for taking our power back, even when we feel wounded by a betrayal from another.

What do our expectations *do* to us? How do our expectations cause us to act, think, and feel? If we let our disappointment from unmet expectations throw us into anger or paralyze us with fear, we become victims of our own feelings. If they leave us stuck in our negative emotions, they are not supporting us in living our best life. If they leave us relying on a specific outcome, we are setting ourselves up for disappointment and ultimately blocking our own peace of mind. Will certain circumstances throw us into having expectations? Absolutely. Yet, the power is within each of us to make the decision to stay stuck in our disappointment or move through our feelings into a more empowered place. We can choose to feel disappointed for a matter of moments or we can choose to stay stuck for hours, days, weeks, or years. How do you want to spend your time? Bemoaning an unfavorable outcome or living your best life?

Here are some examples of everyday expectations. How would you respond?

- You are driving on the highway to an important job interview. Ahead in the distance, you see that traffic has come to a complete stop due to construction. It dawns on you that you that you will be late because you knew you were cutting it close on time anyway. What happens next? The average person would become irritated or feel stressed. You might spend your time yelling at the other cars around you or just simmering in your frustration. What were you expecting? Were you expecting to get there on time even though you got a late start? Were you expecting to get there on time even though there was construction? Were you expecting the construction to be completed? Were you expecting all of the other cars to just pull over and let you go by? What does your frustration do to improve the situation?

- You ask your husband to take out the trash. He says he will. Three hours later, you walk into the kitchen and there is all of the trash sitting by the back door. You are annoyed. The next morning, the trash is still sitting there. What happens to your state of mind? Do you secretly fume about how irresponsible he is? Do you pick a fight? Do you huff and puff and storm around slamming cupboards? Do you build evidence about what an awful person he is? What are your expectations doing to you? Does having expectations change whether or not the trash was taken out--or do your expectations simply rattle you?

- You have worked really hard for the last five years proving yourself to the management team at work. There is an entry level management position open and you believe that you deserve it after all of the ways you have proven yourself. When the time comes, management offers the position to someone else. What were you expecting and how do your expectations impact you? Do you slack off because you feel unappreciated? Do you resent the people who passed you over? Do you withdraw into yourself and take it personally? Or, do you take action to find out what must happen in order for you to get promoted?

> You are married with two children. You and your spouse have very busy careers, full social schedules, and volunteer on the children's sport teams. By any definition, you look like you are the picturesque family, but you know you and your spouse have been drifting apart. One day, your spouse tells you that your marriage is over. You feel blindsided. Clearly, you are stunned at first, but then what? As the reality and disappointment set in, what happens next over the course of the next several months? What were you expecting in the marriage and what are you expecting now?

These are varying degrees of expectations and the impact on our lives would be vastly different. I use these examples, not to minimize an event as significant as the end of a marriage, but to show that expectations show up in our lives in a variety of ways. The end of a marriage can be very traumatic. Yet, the road to reclaiming happiness is through reclaiming personal power and not relying on someone else to give us our happiness back.

Let go of ALL of your disempowering expectations of what you think others should do or outcomes you think should happen, because your expectations only negatively impact you. They set *you* up to get stuck in your own emotions! Do not expect other people to do exactly what you want them to do because you only control yourself. They get to choose what they do. Do not hinge your well being on the actions of someone else. When we live in our expectations of others or of circumstances outside the realm of our control, we are setting ourselves up to be disappointed. We only get to choose what we do and how we respond to any circumstance. We are responsible for our choices. If we know that there is a possibility of ending up stuck in negative emotions, what makes us choose to let expectations of an outcome decide our fate?

> *In the grand scheme of life, we cannot control what other people do. We must learn how to be responsible for our lives, no matter what decisions other people make.*

Unspoken Expectations

Earlier, I mentioned that expectations can be spoken or unspoken. We often get into expecting others to do what we want them to do without even telling them. We believe that they *should* just know what we want. In the case of the impending birthday, you thought your friends should know what you wanted without conveying your wishes or desires. When expectations are unspoken, we are setting up the other person as well as ourselves. We are setting them up for a no-win situation. This is very common in families and in other close relationships. We make assumptions that the other person knows us so well that they should know what we need. It is not an effective way to maintain healthy relationships. In fact, it can lead to destruction. How can they know what we want if we are not willing to tell them?

We must be willing to communicate our needs and we must be willing to do that without expectations attached. We do this by speaking up and clearly, concisely asking for what we want. We can ask for action. We can request information or feedback. We can influence through reason. We can negotiate. We can open lines of communication. We can motivate. If we have positional authority, we can even demand, or institute consequences for inaction. Just *do not get caught up in attaching to disempowering expectations!*

A Comment on Parenting

As a Life Coach, I often hear the question, "As a parent, how can I not have expectations of my children? I want them to behave properly. I want them to have good manners. I want them to excel in life. I have to have expectations of them, or they won't have any for themselves. What do I do?" Even with children, expectations of others still set us up for disappointment. They create the potential for each of us to get stuck in our own negative emotions. As a parent, I would not consciously choose to get stuck in my negative emotions while I am with my children. I would not consciously choose to be frustrated, angry, or stressed out as a result of my expectations. I know that I cannot be the best parent I can be when my thinking is clouded by frustration. Does it happen? Sure, but as my skills increase, my focus on what kind of parent I want to be increases. I am a much more effective parent when I am proactive, not reactive. I am a much better parent when I am focused on mentoring, leading by example, and asking for what I want instead of yelling about what I don't want. I am a better parent when I act on my commitments instead of my emotions. For parents, it is important that we stay as even keeled as possible.

If we are to stay centered ourselves, whatever we ask of our children must be age appropriate and it must be a request. If our child does not comply, as a parent we can choose to institute consequences. We can also model the types of behaviors we want our children to have. We can teach them right from wrong. We can share the benefits of our experiences. We can praise and anticipate. What we really want to do is inspire them to strive for excellence and to expand their possibilities. Children who learn how to take responsibility for their actions and make better choices on their own, develop more self-esteem and feel more in control of their lives as adults. The more we can help develop self-esteem in our children, the more they will create their own anticipations for an abundant future. In order to do that, we must keep our expectations in check.

Disempowering Emotions are a Call to Action

Sometimes it is challenging to see when you have expectations. Often, we do not notice our expectations, until our feelings reveal them. Our emotions are an internal compass and they offer great insight into ourselves. Our emotions reveal the state of our thinking and show us when we have expectations. Here are some additional red flag emotions that reveal unmet expectations:

Feelings that reveal disempowering expectations:

Obligated	Agitated	Angry	Annoyed
Trapped	Grumpy	Used	Betrayed
Enraged	Appalled	Shunned	Irritated
Victimized	Fearful	Worried	Blamed
Entitled	Deserted	Distressed	Judged
Disappointed	Resentful	Tricked	Outraged
Mistreated	Stressed	Tense	Guilty
Overworked	Shamed	Spiteful	Humiliated
Entitled	Disgusted	Powerless	Wronged
Disrespected	Frustrated	Anxious	Bitter
Critical	Helpless	Vengeful	Devastated

Anytime we feel angry, enraged, or bitter, we had an unfulfilled expectation. Anytime we feel frustrated, critical, or disappointed, we had an expectation. Anytime we feel resentful, betrayed, or taken for granted, we had an expectation. Even fear, itself, is based in the expectation that we will experience discomfort or pain.

Our behaviors towards others also reveal our expectations. Judging others is a sign of expecting other people to do things in the way you believe they should be done. Similarly, comparing yourself to others brings up expectations of you or of other people. Trying to control others, manipulating, or shaming others into doing what you want them to do, all have expectations entangled in them.

If you are anxious and worry, you have expectations and the worry is about not getting the result you want. If you whine, complain, and feel sorry for yourself, you think things should be different than they are. If you feel betrayed, wronged, or mistreated, you have expectations that life should be fair and just. If you are defensive, you are protecting your perception of what you think should be. If you feel guilty, you have expectations about yourself and what you thought you should have done. Again, it is natural to have feelings, but we must remember that we do not want to get stuck here. To live our best life, we must decide to work through our feelings and make more empowering choices.

Blame is another expectation that we use as a fear response. When we are dissatisfied with our lives, it is easy to choose to point the finger at someone else or blame our circumstances. It is also avoiding taking responsibility to move forward. If you are blaming someone or something, you are not taking responsibility for your life. Even if you are stuck in blaming yourself, you are not taking responsibility for the things you can do right now to change your life. You are either taking full responsibility or you are not. Blame focuses on the past, responsibility looks forward toward change. No matter how much you blame yourself or someone else, it will not change you or the situation. Choose to focus on possible solutions, not the problem. If you find yourself blaming, it is a call to action to be more responsible. All negative emotions are a *call to action.*

Ask yourself these questions:

> What am I not facing right now?
>
> What expectations am I harboring?
>
> What can I do to change my current situation?
>
> How can I regain responsibility for my life?

In the case of the traffic, you can plan better, leave earlier, or notify them that you will be late, but you cannot control the amount of traffic on the road. Staying stuck in your frustration does not get you there any faster. You can follow up with your husband and ask when he plans to take out the trash, but fuming about it only hurts you. You can work hard and ask for the promotion, but ultimately you do not get to decide if you get it. Again, expectations are based upon your perception of what you think "should" happen. You are expecting other people to do what you want; you are expecting to have things go your way; you are expecting yourself to attain a certain standard; you are expecting to get what you want. If things work out, you are fine. If things do not work out, you are the one who pays the price. Disempowering expectations set you up every time! Don't do it to yourself. Release your expectations and your attachment to the outcome.

For me, experiencing a negative emotion heightens my awareness. It is a red flag that it is time for me to look at myself and my expectations. Feeling off center is a wake up call for me to ask myself, "I recognize that I am feeling disappointed or frustrated right now, so what was I expecting from someone, something, or from the situation? What do I have control over right now and what do I not have control over? Who do I choose to be right now?" Asking myself these questions shifts my thinking into being proactive, instead of reactive.

I believe that all negative emotions are a call to action. As I said, they are a guide to our internal compass and inner wisdom. They are like signposts that reveal the possible paths open to us. We can choose to stay on the same path and experience the same feelings or we can choose a new path. Negative emotions can serve a purpose as long as we use them to propel us forward instead of staying stuck in them. The time that it takes for each of us to move forward depends where we are in our life journey and the challenges we are facing. As we master the skills of facing our fears, trusting our intuition, and releasing our expectations, we gain more mastery over our emotions. When we decide to use our emotions as a springboard to take action in a positive direction, we grow by leaps and bounds.

> Negative emotions are a call to action. They are sign posts that reveal when it is time to release expectations and change course.

What we are really talking about is being accountable for our true responsibilities and letting go of responsibilities that are not ours. We control ourselves, but we do not get to control what other people say, think, or do. Taking ownership of our personal responsibility, and releasing all else, is the foundation for the Law of Responsibility.

The Law of Responsibility

The starting point of true freedom and happiness lies in accepting full and complete responsibility for our lives. Remember our thoughts ultimately create our reality. We cannot always control the events or circumstances we are faced with, but we can control how we respond to them. We are responsible for our thoughts, feelings, words, and deeds. We are responsible for our actions or in-actions. We are responsible for our own internal balance and being true to what our inner wisdom tells us. We cannot hear our inner wisdom when our minds are cluttered with expectations or emotional baggage. We must work through our feelings in order to create our best life. We know we do not see life as clearly when we are looking through the eyes of anger versus looking through the eyes of joy.

We are responsible for our own happiness and our emotions, regardless of what other people do. In other words, we cannot hold someone or something else responsible for our life. Our feelings are our responsibility. Our choices are our responsibility. No one else is responsible for our life or our happiness—not our spouse, significant other, parents, siblings, friends, co-workers, no one. We must be accountable for creating the life we want. It is completely within our control to decide the course of our life on a daily basis. Each of us has our own free will and free will enables us to be responsible for ourselves. When we are responsible, we are accountable for every decision and we proactively do things because we want to, not because we are supposed to, ought to, have to, or should.

We are responsible for saying no when we mean no and yes when we mean yes. We are fully and completely responsible for conveying our wants, needs, and desires to those around us. We are responsible for asking for what we want. We cannot expect someone else to know what we really want if we are not willing to ask for it. We cannot expect someone else to read our minds.

We are responsible for understanding that our boundaries, values, needs, and priorities may be different from our parents, our siblings, our significant other, or anyone else. We must be clear on what we consider important and separate ourselves from being bound or influenced by the values of others. Just because they may not see something as important, does not minimize the value to us. For example, I know that I must have some quiet, creative time each day in order to feel centered. I need time, space, and stillness. My husband does not have that same need. He can work in the midst of chaos and not even notice what is going on around him. In our relationship, we make a conscious effort to respect each other's needs and make sure those needs are being met. So, in order to be responsible, we must stand steadfastly in our own values and desires. We must be accountable for taking care of ourselves.

> *We are responsible for our own happiness and our emotions, regardless of what other people do. In other words, we cannot hold someone or something else responsible for our life. Our feelings are our responsibility. Our choices are our responsibility.*

The Law of Responsibility serves as a reminder that there is a balance between giving and receiving in relationships. Those of us who have a strong desire to help others may develop an exaggerated sense of responsibility where we assume too much responsibility for other people. It is based in a desire to assist and give to others, but it can be at the expense of our own needs. This debilitates us as well as the person or persons we want to help. When we assume excess responsibility, we sacrifice our own needs and we rob others of the experience of learning how to handle challenges on their own. When we take on too much responsibility, balance eventually wins out at the expense of our well being or at the expense of the relationship. We cannot be responsible for someone else's well being and they cannot be responsible for ours.

Samantha's Story

Samantha and her husband Bryan decided to relocate their family to a new state. When their house sold, Samantha was thrilled to take house hunting trips and make plans for her future. They found a lovely home in a lovely community, but they were now going to be two time zones away from the rest of Samantha's family. She knew she would miss her family and still, she was excited for the adventure they were about to embark upon. Her life over the next few months was totally consumed with packing, organizing, and planning.

After they had moved and settled in to their new environment, Samantha started to feel a little homesick, especially around any holidays. She and her family were very happy in their new community and did not regret their choice to move. Yet, she was noticing some changes in her relationships with her hometown family. She used to talk to her family on the phone four times a day, now it was maybe four times a month. The emotional distance tugged at her heart strings and when she tried to connect with them, she felt as if they were distant and uninterested in her new life. She wanted them to visit, but they never put effort into making plans.

Samantha felt hurt, rejected, and even angry. She felt like they had all just cut her off because she had moved away. She tried to tell herself that she didn't need them anyway, but her heart ached for them to call her. She wanted them to call, to fly into town, or to ask her to come home. She wanted them to miss her. They didn't even try to stop her from moving. They didn't ask her to stay. They didn't try to keep in touch. She thought that they must not have loved her the way she thought they did. She believed she was always the black sheep of the family and this validated her position. Samantha had expectations and she was building evidence. She was in fear and she had given her power away.

As we talked, I asked Samantha several questions about the difference between her family's current behavior and their past behavior. She said her mom and dad were real home bodies. They had some fear of flying and rarely went anywhere. Her brother and his family had some financial challenges and they were juggling two jobs in order to reduce their debt. Samantha acknowledged that she and her brother did not talk about her decision to move prior to their house selling. I continued to ask Samantha many questions because I knew that her inner wisdom would give her the answers that she was seeking. I asked Samantha to write her expectations down.

Here are some that she wrote:

I expected them to respond a certain way: to be upset that I was moving.

I expected our relationship to stay the same even though I moved away.

I expected them to call me more.

I expected them to fly.

I expected them to make plans to visit me.

Then I asked her to list what she is responsible for next to each expectation.

She wrote:

I expected them to respond a certain way: to be upset that I was moving.

I am responsible only for my own emotional state and I am responsible for sharing my needs.

I expected our relationship to stay the same even though I moved away.

I am responsible for changing the relationship when I decided to move. I can be responsible for seeking creative ways to keep in touch or I can accept that our relationship will be different.

I expected them to call me more.

I am responsible for asking for what I want or for taking action with no strings attached.

I expected them to fly, knowing they are afraid.

I am responsible for accepting them for who they are, not expecting them to change.

I expected them to make plans to visit me.

I am responsible for making a specific request. I am responsible for being willing to hear their position.

Samantha had been caught up in her disempowering expectations. She blamed her family for the changes in their relationship. Once she saw that she could take responsibility, she was able to let go of her disappointment and take charge of her feelings again. Samantha decided to be more proactive and every time she felt a disempowering expectation, she saw it for what it was--a roadblock to her happiness. She took responsibility for her role and her choices. She followed her intuition and opened the door for heart to heart dialogue with her family. She learned so much when she asked what they were thinking and feeling, instead of assuming and building evidence. Releasing her expectations and taking responsibility for her choices brought her peace of mind. She was no longer the victim of her feelings, but a woman in charge of her own happiness.

Take Charge through Responsibility

The Law of Responsibility states that we are responsible for our lives. We are responsible for our choices, our thoughts, our feelings, our actions and our in-actions. We are responsible for listening to our inner wisdom and for following our own internal compass to find our own proper point of balance. When we nurture ourselves and determine the boundaries of our personal responsibility to ourselves, we can then create more harmony when giving to others. In order to live our best life, we must look within and be fully responsible for our choices and the way we interact in the world.

Being responsible for your life equates to emotional maturity. Self-reliance, self-control, and autonomy are all signs of emotional maturity and responsibility. Symptoms of irresponsibility are self-pity, co-dependence, pessimism, avoiding reality, fear, aimlessness, self-righteousness, blaming, and excuses. Yes, we are all human beings. Part of being human is experiencing the vast variety of human emotions. We all have moments of feeling disempowered. Yet, true maturity is the ability to recognize the feeling, choose to be responsible for it, and choose to take action in a new direction. Notice I used the word "ability". Moving through disempowering emotions and moving into personal responsibility is a skill. It takes awareness and practice.

There are several essential conditions for lasting change. You must create awareness that something needs to change and you must a have willingness to take action. You also must accept that you are where you are because of you. You are the captain of your ship. If your ship is in shallow water or has run aground, you played a role in getting to where you are. Conversely, if you are on course, you also played a role. You are free to choose your thoughts and feelings. Therefore, you must accept the consequences of what you think and how you feel. Every time you experience a negative emotion, it is an opportunity to grow. It is an opportunity to choose to learn how to take a new action.

We can release our disempowering expectations and emotions, by focusing on taking responsibility for our lives. Turn expectations into personal responsibility. Say, "I cannot control every situation; I can only control my response to it." Let go of the way you think things should be and take responsibility for the reality of your life. Embrace what is, not what you think *should* be. The day you take complete responsibility for your life is the day you really start living. Your happiness no longer depends on what other people do; it depends on what *you* do. Your peace of mind no longer depends on whether your expectations are met or not; you take charge of your life and become responsible for your choices. When your focus is on being responsible for you, life no longer happens to you. You create your life.

People who feel a sense of achievement in their life have a strong sense of personal accountability and responsibility. They show us over and over again that it is not what happens in life, but how we respond to what happens that matters. They hold themselves accountable for the quality of their lives. Achievers face problems and challenges, but they don't give themselves permission to pass off blame or responsibility to someone else. They don't spend their time accusing, confronting, or being angry because they know that being responsible for their thoughts and actions is the key to moving forward. When you get stuck in disempowering emotions, you give all of your peace and power away.

> *When your focus is on being responsible for you, life no longer happens to you. You create your life.*

Locus of Control

The degree to which you feel positive about your life is proportional to how much you feel you have control over your destiny. In psychology, this is called the "locus of control". An internal locus of control correlates with a high degree of self-satisfaction, no matter the circumstances of your life. In other words, if you take responsibility for all of your thoughts, actions, words, and deeds, you will have a higher degree of satisfaction. A higher degree of self-satisfaction also correlates with a higher degree of self-esteem. People with a high internal locus of control use language that starts with "I". They take responsibility for their lives and use phrases such as "I think, I feel, and I choose".

On the other hand, if you have an external locus of control, you operate more under the belief that you have little control over what happens in your life. You feel more controlled by some external force, person, or situation. You have the perception that outside influences control you and you are at the mercy of what other people do. People with a high external locus of control assign responsibility externally. They might say things like "My job is…, My friends do…, or Things are…" Most experts agree that anxiety, stress, worry, and psychosomatic illness come about as a result of people feeling like they have little or no control in some aspect of their life.

There is a correlation with the external locus of control and disempowering expectations in that we believe our happiness or well being is determined by sources outside of ourselves. In addition, the net result of the feelings is the same. For example, being in debt, feeling stuck in a bad relationship, or loss of a job, typically bring up feelings such as anxiety, feeling victimized, or feeling powerless. These are also fear based feelings. The reality is you do have control over your life. You get to choose how much money you spend. You choose whether you stay in a relationship or not. You do have the ability to shift your power and your choices. You can speak up and ask for what you want. You can decide to act on your commitments or act on your emotions.

Emotions are transient. They come and they go. They change based upon your perspective. They are a gauge of where you are emotionally at any given moment. The only meaning and power any feeling can ever have is the meaning and power you give to it. You can choose to move through the feeling into a more empowering place. The overall goal is to focus on an internal locus of control, act with responsibility, and release disempowering expectations. How can you tell if you are on the right track? Ask yourself these questions:

Expectations or Responsibility

1. Are your emotions empowering or disempowering you?
2. Is "should" or "have to" a part of your thinking or your vocabulary?
3. Are you attached to a specific outcome?
4. Are you attempting to control something or someone that is out of your control?
5. Are you being responsible for your happiness or are you making someone else responsible for your happiness?
6. Are you focused on what you can do right now?

As we move from expectation to personal responsibility, we will begin to notice some shifts in our thinking and our emotions. When we get caught up in our expectations, our emotions show up as anger, disappointment, or some other negative emotion. We focus outside of ourselves and essentially seek to place blame on someone or something by making them responsible for our happiness. Moving through our negative emotions brings a sense of enlightenment because we often discover that we really were upset with our own choices all along. This is our opportunity to learn and gain wisdom from the experience.

If we were back in that traffic jam on our way to an interview, we are probably not really upset with the traffic, but with ourselves for not planning better. If we spent hours upon hours fuming about the trash not being taken out, we were probably upset with ourselves for wasting so much time being angry about garbage or for not simply asking for what we wanted, even if we had to ask again. If we were upset that our friends did not remember our birthday, we could have reached out to them and celebrated anyway. Our natural state is one of love, peace, connection, and compassion. When we choose to be reactive as a result of unfulfilled expectations, we are pulling away from that natural state.

We all have the ability to choose to take responsibility for our lives. We might think that we are victims of circumstance and have all kinds of evidence about how we were wronged, treated unfairly, or disrespected. We might even believe that we have every right to be angry and convince others to join in on our opinion. Self-righteousness and justifications do nothing to move us forward. They keep us stuck thinking that we were right when being right does not bring us happiness. They keep us stuck in our problems and in our misery. Placing blame does not empower us; taking responsibility does. Responsibility focuses on the present and the future. It moves us to "I have learned and next time, I will make a different choice". Responsibility gives us a sense of self-reliance and control over our future.

Action for Life Exercise:

Make a list of all of the times you notice you are angry, annoyed, irritated, frustrated, or disappointed over the next week. Write down what you were expecting. Below that, write down what you are responsible for. How does taking responsibility feel? What do you want to do differently in the future?

Make of list of anyone from your past or present that you harbor a grudge or feel angry at. Write down what you are responsible for in each situation. If this situation is still bothering you, how can you take charge of your life? What can you do to support your own needs?

If you were to take full responsibility for your life, what is one thing that you would start doing? What is one thing you would stop doing?

Action for Life Team:

Who will support you in being responsible for your choices?

When you are upset, who can you vent to? Once you vent, you must be willing to take responsibility and then release your expectations. You cannot repeat events again and again. No dwelling on it. Decide how you will move forward.

Chapter Strategy

Use expectations to expand your horizons without attaching to an outcome. Release disempowering expectations and take full personal responsibility for creating your life.

Chapter 3 Key Points

- You and only you are responsible for your life.

- Law of Expectations: whatever we believe or expect is possible becomes our reality.

- Empowering expectations uplift us and push us beyond our perceived limitations. They raise our anticipations of what is possible.

- Disempowering expectations attempt to control other people, situations, or outcomes.

- Disempowering expectations always set us up to get stuck in negative emotions if our expectations are unfulfilled.

- Negative emotions are a call to action.

- The Law of Responsibility shows us that we are responsible for our thoughts, feelings, and actions.

- Turn your expectations into personal responsibility by saying, "I am responsible for…"

- Do not assume that others can read your mind. Ask for what you want.

- Embrace the reality of what is, not what you think things should be.

- When you are responsible for your life, your happiness is determined by you and only you. Personal responsibility is personal freedom.

Chapter 4

There is ALWAYS a Choice.

"Whatever the mind of man can conceive and believe, it can achieve."

--Napoleon Hill

Everything we think is our choice. Everything we say or do is up to us. Everything we are or ever will be is decided by our choices. Everything we experience today is the culmination of all of the choices we have made in the past. Everything we will experience tomorrow will be decided by our choices. Our choices are limitless. We can choose to be proactive when we face a challenge or we can choose to be reactive. We can choose to take action or we can choose to stay where we are. We can choose to make changes today or postpone them until tomorrow.

Whatever we choose, we must be willing to take responsibility for our choices. If we choose to rely on others opinions instead of trusting our intuition, we are making a choice. If we choose to let other people make our decisions for us, we are making a choice. If we choose to allow our past to dictate our future, we are making a choice. Each and every day, we each get to decide what we are willing to accept and what we are willing to do.

The Law of Choices

Once you are clear that you are responsible for your life, you can begin to make more empowering choices. As we have already discussed, when you let the disappointment of unmet expectations impact your balance, your center, and your happiness, you are allowing external forces to run your life. Disempowering expectations make someone or something else responsible for your happiness and well being. You are essentially choosing to be at the mercy of whatever comes your way in life. You have probably heard before that we either create or allow everything that happens in our lives. If you are not making the choices that propel you forward, you are choosing to stay where you are. With every thought, feeling, and behavior, you are choosing either

To stay stagnant	→	To grow
To disempower yourself	→	To empower yourself
To live in fear	→	To live in love
To view life as against you	→	To view life as for you
To be reactive	→	To be proactive
To take negative action	→	To take positive action

As you can see, our choices are not necessarily made by what we say, but by what actions we take or do not take. Our actions are the results of our thoughts and choices. We can choose to take charge of our life or allow our life to take charge of our choices. We want to be able to shift our thinking and actions from an external focus to an internal focus in order to reclaim our personal power.

Our choices are unlimited. We choose what we have for dinner, where we live, what we do for a living, and what we do with our time. We do not necessarily have equal choices over circumstances, but we all have infinite choices. For example, a wheel chair bound person does not have the same life choices as someone who is able bodied; a person born in a third world country may not have the same choices as someone born in an industrialized nation; and a person who is financially poor does not have the same choices as a wealthy person. In the grand scheme, your circumstances do not matter. Choice is about how we respond to the circumstances we have. As our circumstances change, our choices can change. All of our lives, we all have the ability to make choices.

As we are deciding what choices to make, there are two primary forces at work within each of us: the voice of fear and the voice of inner wisdom or love. The voice of inner wisdom wants us to make decisions based upon our commitments, intuition, and self-trust. The voice of fear wants us to make decisions based upon doing anything possible to stay emotionally safe. Fear feels like an internal scramble to take cover. When we are in fear, our choices are frequently made by impulses, defenses, and knee jerk reactions. Fear often causes us to become defensive or to place blame outside of ourselves in order to deflect the attention away from ourselves and to manipulate us into thinking that we have no choices. No matter what our voice of fear says, we *always* have a choice. With each choice that we make, we create results.

> *Choice is about how we respond to the circumstances we have. As our circumstances change, our choices can change. All of our lives, we all have the ability to make choices.*

The Law of Integrity

As I inferred in the last chapter, when we move through our negative feelings and find the way back to our true center or natural state of being, we often discover that we are actually upset with ourselves, not with another, for the choices that we have made. Again, life is a journey and a learning process. There is no right or wrong feeling. Feelings are simply a gauge showing us where we are. When we find that we are upset with ourselves, we discover that we have not listened to our inner wisdom, our intuition, and our internal compass. Our impulses or fears have led the way.

The Law of Integrity confirms that we must strive to live as our true self following the calling on our inner wisdom and personal compass in order to live our best life. Integrity is being integrated: knowing who we are, being who we are, and acting on our highest values and beliefs, despite any urges or manipulations from fear to act to the contrary. Integrity is thinking, speaking, behaving, and interacting in a way that is consistent with our authentic self. It is not about pretending to be perfect or flawless. It is about truly accepting all of who we are, acknowledging our weaknesses while using our strengths to light the path for ourselves and others. People are natural imitators. When we act as our true self, our inner gifts shine through. When we shine our light, we inspire others to do the same.

Our natural state of being is that of peace, love, contentment, and inner joy. If you look into the eyes of a young child, you see wonder, curiosity, and happiness. Children are born showing their authentic self. It is our fears, self-defeating expectations, and negative emotions that move us away from that state. When we allow love, not fear, to guide us, we find our inner wisdom. Our inner wisdom is our guide. It is our intuition and internal compass. We have a moral compass that knows what is right for us and what is wrong for us. We have a behavioral compass that guides our body language, our words, and our actions. We have a thought compass that influences our thinking. When we listen to our internal compasses, we are on the path to our natural state of being. We are happy with ourselves and feel a sense of pride in our choices.

Recently, we went on our yearly vacation to the beach. My eleven year old son was walking with his cousin from our rental house to the beach when they came upon a man in a wheel chair. The man was trying to push himself up the sidewalk toward the beach ramp. He struggled because thick sand had blown onto the cement making his wheels hard to turn. My son, who is relatively shy around strangers stopped and asked the man if he would like some help. At first, the man declined, but then continued to struggle. My son asked again and the man agreed. So, my son, who is about 5'5" and weighs less than 100 pounds, grabbed the handles and began to push the wheel chair through the sand toward the ramp. The man was very grateful and my son felt very good about himself.

I got to the beach a few minutes after this had transpired and I could see that my son was beaming. He explained to me what he had done and I gave him praise for being so proactive and for helping another person in need. I also asked him to tell me all about how he felt about himself. He was proud that he helped someone in need; he was proud that he had the strength to push the man through the sand; and he was proud that he spoke up and offered help instead of walking past the man. I asked my son to remember the feelings that went along with his small act of kindness because when we choose to move through life doing what we know our inner wisdom wants us to do, our life is filled with pride, joy, and self-confidence.

If fear had kept my son from speaking up and offering help, I suspect that in the moment he would not have felt very good about himself. He would have gone on with his day, but I believe that all of these moments, when we know our heart wants us to make one choice and we make another, add up in our psyche. When we show up in the world acting out of alignment with our integrity, subtle energy forces are set into motion. We begin to justify reasons for betraying the calling of our heart. We begin to let fear take control, detach from our true self, and isolate ourselves from connecting with humanity. Let's talk about another example.

> *Integrity is being integrated: knowing who we are, being who we are, and acting on our highest values and beliefs, despite any urges or manipulations from fear to act to the contrary.*

Michael's Story

Michael was a successful salesman, husband, and father of two young boys. He had just been hired away from another company and promoted to a new management position at a market competitor. He wanted this promotion very much, but once he had accepted the position, his voice of fear was telling him that he had better prove himself quickly. He was on edge. He had a team of six sales representatives assigned to him. They all had acceptable sales numbers, but Michael wanted to look like a star in the eyes of upper management and he pushed his team hard with very high expectations.

He spent hour after hour pouring over sales figures. He lost sleep at night consumed by his desire to raise his sales percentages. When members of his team came to him with a challenge, all he could think about was that a challenge will impede sales. He did not want to hear about their circumstances or their excuses. "Make it happen", was his mantra. He spent his time looking at paperwork, thinking of strategies to boost sales. Michael worked long hours. He often missed dinner with his family and his son's soccer games. When Michael's manager asked how things were going, Michael became very defensive because he felt like his manager was judging his abilities.

A few months went by and the sales numbers were not improving. Michael began to resent some of his sales team members because he saw them as lazy or incompetent. Here he was working so hard, investing countless hours into succeeding and his people were being lazy. Michael also felt disconnected from his manager. He felt like his manager was uninvolved in his team's drive for success. When Michael went to a sales meeting, he listened silently in the back of the room and then brooded because the meeting took so much time away from the field. The close of the fiscal year was coming up fast.

Life at home was not going well. His sons went on their way, getting rides to and from their soccer practice. They barely said hello to Michael when they saw him. Michael's wife was getting used to him not being around either. She now got into the habit of expecting him to grab dinner at work because that is what he did so often.

One day as Michael was ordering take out food for another dinner at his desk, two of his sales representatives were waiting outside the door to his office. They came in one at a time to each lay their letter of resignation on his desk. Michael thought, "You can't leave me now. I won't make my numbers for the year." As each representative explained their reasons, Michael was dumbfounded. He took their resignations hard.

Instead of staying at work that day, he decided to go home for dinner. While he was driving home, all he could think about was how much time and effort he had put into making his team a success. "Those ungrateful reps will never work for another manager as committed as I am", he thought. When he got home, the house was empty. Michael wondered where his family was and why they were not there when he needed them most. He felt abandoned and started to think about all of the times he was there for them and how selfish they were for not being there for him. A few minutes later, the phone rang and it was Michael's manager calling to ask what happened to stimulate two resignations. Michael explained, placed blame, and made a myriad of excuses, but his manager still seemed baffled about why two long time employees would just leave. After Michael hung up the phone, he again felt defensive and mentally reviewed a long list of things his manager could have done to be more supportive. Michael's life was not going the way he wanted it to and it was time to change direction. Michael hired me as his Life Coach.

As Michael and I began to work through some of his feelings, he discovered a whole host of expectations. As usual, I had him assign his own personal responsibility to each expectation. Taking responsibility was very enlightening to him and his perspective started to shift. I did not want Michael to get caught in the trap of reviewing "could have, would have and should have" over and over in his mind, but I wanted him to gain some awareness of how his choices created his reality. I asked him several questions about how the voice of fear and how the voice of inner wisdom played into his choices. He started to see that he had, in fact, ignored his inner wisdom. His fear kept him blaming and judging others instead of looking at himself. By ignoring his inner wisdom, he started to see himself as a faultless victim who worked tirelessly and was taken for granted. At the same time, he built evidence that those around him were lazy, ungrateful, uninvolved, judgmental, and unsupportive.

When we talked specifically about his actions or inactions, I asked him what his inner wisdom was telling him. The follow are some of the things he wrote.

My inner wisdom told me to:

Listen to the challenges my reps faced and support them in creating solutions

Work with my reps instead of spending all my time pouring over the numbers

Connect with them as human beings instead of seeing them as a means to a result

Ask my manger for guidance instead of acting like a maverick

Focus on quality training and daily steps instead of outcomes

Be present in the moment at the sales meetings in order to gain knowledge

Make time for the family I value so much

So, by betraying himself and not listening to his internal compass, he built evidence against others and he disconnected himself from his team, his manager, and his family. It was easy to make them bad and make himself a victim. It was easy to make assumptions about their actions and exaggerate their perceived faults. He also assigned labels to everyone else based upon how he perceived the situation. "They" became selfish, lazy, incompetent, and ungrateful people. The dynamics for this entire scenario started in Michael's thoughts. He wanted to achieve success and prove himself, an admirable goal, but he made choices based upon his voice of fear, not his voice of inner wisdom.

When we are willing to take a good look at ourselves, we can see that our choices begin with our thoughts. We can discern whether it is fear or inner wisdom guiding those choices. Every choice continues on to impact our actions and creates our reality.

Even our choices to act on our emotions or act on our commitments play a significant role in how we create our lives. When we betray ourselves by not listening to our inner wisdom, we begin to disconnect from the humanity of others. We begin to see others as objects, with little intelligence or feelings. We build evidence to tear them down and build ourselves up. Once again, there are great lessons when we experience negative emotions. These moments can guide us back to our true selves, our intuition, and our inner wisdom. They can give us perspective about who we want to be in this world, how we want to show up, how we want to treat others, and what we feel like when we are not true to ourselves.

Our choices may lead to different paths. We can choose the path of resistance, where we may face many hurdles, or we can choose the path of our inner compass. No matter what path we choose, the path will always lead us back to the lessons that we must learn in order to live our best life.

> *When we choose to betray our own inner wisdom, we choose to disconnect from others, build evidence against them, and avoid taking responsibility for our own actions.*

Excuses and Denial

When we betray our own inner wisdom and integrity, we are, in essence, creating excuses to avoid responsibility for our actions. Excuses also show up in our lives in several other ways. We use traumatic events to avoid moving forward. We use excuses when we procrastinate or blame. We use excuses by building evidence for all of the reasons we can't make changes or make effective use of our time. Remember Elizabeth, the woman who was afraid to be vulnerable? She was sure that the past would repeat itself, that her relationships would end in loss, and then she made excuses about how the men she dated were all "jerks". Excuses are *always* feelings based, not fact based. We use excuses to validate our position, to sooth our ego, and to avoid taking responsibility for our life.

In the big picture of life, "I can't" means "I can. I just don't want to apply effort." We don't want to because it requires risk, focus, and the discomfort of stepping outside of our comfort zone. Stepping outside of our comfort zone brings up fear. Yet, not stepping out of our comfort zone has huge implications for our overall self-esteem and quality of life. Excuses are the enemy of personal responsibility, action, and peace of mind. When we live in our excuses, we do not feel responsible or accountable for our lives. Even the biggest, best, most justified excuse can never feel as good as the smallest success. You are the only person that is in charge of making choices that bring you happiness and fulfillment. You must make the choice to do it for yourself.

The Principle of Intention

Sometimes we feel like our choices are made for us because we are bound in duty. At some point you have probably said, "I have to do this. I don't have a choice." Yet, in reality, you are making a choice. It is you're your choice to view whatever you are doing as an obligation. You could say, "I choose to do this because it is the right thing to do." Or you could say, "I choose not to do this and I will be responsible for the consequences of my choice." Even though we are not always aware of it, we are making choices all day long and each choice has a consequence. Each choice has feelings attached to it. If your choice is to live by what you think you "should" do, chances are, you feel like your life is controlling you instead of you being in charge of your life. If you make choices from a place of "I choose", then you will feel you have more control over your life and destiny. You will not feel obligated, but empowered because you have made the choice consciously and purposely. Any time you take an action based on conscious choice, you are taking an action based on the Principle of Intention.

An intention is a determination or resolve to take action based on your commitments and values. It is a manifestation of who you are and how you want to show up in the world.

For example, do you want to be the person that blames others for the state of your life, makes excuses, and is reactive? Or do you want to be the person that takes responsibility, is authentic, and takes action based on your commitments? Commitments align with the voice of inner wisdom through intention. Intention is a commitment to acting on your inner compass. "I choose to" and "I intend to" are choices based in intention.

An intention is a conscious action that is designed to inspire and motivate you to move forward to a desired state of being, not just a specific outcome. It is an overall process, a way of doing, and is bigger than any one particular goal or time frame. It is a commitment to a way of being. In other words, it is what you are committed to doing or what you are willing to do. An intention is created by your thoughts, thoughts about what you want to practice doing or becoming. Intentions are the foundation for living your life with purpose and consciously taking steps to create the life you want. Intentions are actions.

Intentional or Non-Intentional Action

What is the difference between intentional versus non-intentional action? Non-intentional action is more of a reaction that results from an emotional response. As we have discussed, all action begins with a thought. Your thought creates an emotion which ultimately leads to an action. Say for example, you hear a song starting on the radio. If it is a song you like, your thought is, "This is a great song." As you hear the song, you feel happy and uplifted. The resulting action might be turning up the volume and singing along with the song. Conversely, if you do not like the song, your thought is, "I do not want to hear this song." The feeling is aversion and the action is that you change the radio station. In both cases, the actions came about as a result of the thought and the associated feeling. It was more of a reaction. You did not put much thought into either action. Your feelings motivated the action. Your feelings created an emotional response. Here is what it looks like:

Non-Intentional Action

Thought→creates Feeling→creates Action→creates Reality

For the sake of clarity, let's talk about another example. You are working on a time-sensitive project at work with another employee. Your boss has assigned the project to both of you, but you are beginning to realize that you are far more committed to the success of the project than the other employee. Two days before the deadline, the other employee calls in sick. You are left alone with a mountain of work to do. You feel the urge to get angry and frustrated. Using the model that we used above, say your thought is, "I will have to just deal with this." Then, the resulting emotion might be feeling burdened and the action might be to assume that the outcome will be less than ideal.

Or, if your thought is, "There is no way I can handle this", your feeling becomes stress. The resulting action might be working around the clock in a panicked, frenzied way. In both cases, your feeling or emotional state plays a significant role in your actions. You are reacting to your thoughts and feelings. You are choosing to let your feelings decide your course of action. This is non-intentional action.

With intentional action, your actions take place in alignment with your commitments, not as a result of your feelings or emotional state. You will still have feelings. Nevertheless, your intentions become the determining factor for the action you take, no matter what the feeling is. Feelings and reactions are essentially taken out of the equation of action. If we used intentional action in the above example, you would choose to focus on your commitment to the completion of the project instead of focusing on your feelings. Your commitment would be doing the best job you can in the time you have. You can acknowledge your feelings, but you take action on your intentions or your commitments. Here is what intentional action looks like:

Intentional Action

Thought→creates Intention→creates Action→creates Reality

Say, your child disobeys you. You feel frustration. Yet, despite feeling frustrated, you choose to act on your commitments. First, you choose to release any disempowering expectations. Then, you choose to take action based on your commitment to the type of parent and role model you want to be. You choose to be a patient mentor. You acknowledge your feelings of frustration and disappointment, but choose to take action based on intention. You may choose to send you child to his room, mentally regroup, and then calmly discuss the issues and consequences with your child.

Or, someone cuts you off in traffic. You have an emotional response of being scared or angry. Instead of acting on your emotional response, you choose to stand by your intention. You choose to act on your commitment to being a responsible driver no matter what the people around you do. Your emotions do not dictate your actions. Your commitments decide and then your emotions follow.

Your boyfriend or girlfriend dumps you and you feel hurt. You still decide to be true to the person that you know you are. You choose not to beat yourself up and to see that every relationship, every experience, is an investment in yourself. You are choosing to live by your intention and commitment to yourself. Yes, it will take some time to move through your feelings, but if you focus on what you are committed to, you will benefit from the experience.

The difference between non-intentional action and intentional action is how you choose to let your feelings influence you. Feelings are a temporary experience. They change as we change. We become more empowered when we can use our thoughts and commitments as our internal compass, instead of our emotions.

Steps to Intentional Action: ACT

1. Acknowledge your feelings
2. Choose commitments over emotions
3. Take action aligned with intention

Unless we put conscious effort into our thoughts and our actions, we are not really committed to living our best life. We are not committed to creating the life we want. We must take responsibility for the directions we choose instead of seeing life as something that just happens to us. When we choose to live our life based upon our intentions and commitments, we are making an investment in our life as well as our own self-esteem. Our self-esteem increases when we feel like we have control over the quality of our lives and when we learn that we can handle whatever comes our way. Acting on our commitments keeps us focused on moving toward our desired results regardless of any bumps in the road. Being proactive and choosing to live by intention builds self-trust, that internal knowing that we can handle anything we are faced with. You create your life by the thoughts you think and the actions you take. You can work towards a desired state of being, instead of a specific outcome. Your thoughts create your intentions; your intentions create your actions; and your actions create your reality.

I strongly encourage you to write down your intentions and repeat them out loud. These actions anchor your commitment with a variety of modalities: visual, kinesthetic, and auditory. When there is congruency in each of these modalities, you create a clearer, focused, internal message. It also creates a higher probability for you to practice the action you are committing to. Again, intentions are action based. They require you to do something or practice an action that moves you toward a desired state of being.

Intentions can be stated in a variety of ways, but the basic components are the same. Personally, I have found "I am willing to" and "I commit to" to be the most useful and inspiring ways to write intentions. To me, they inspire both commitment and curiosity. If you are curious, you want to take action and explore the possibilities. Choose what works best for you.

> *Intentions inspire you to work toward a desired state of being, not a specific outcome.*

The basic components of intentions:

- Start with "I"—I am willing, I will, I am committed to, I commit to, I intend to, I choose to
- Action based, includes a verb, and inspires you to DO something
- Show commitment to how you want to show up in the world, who you want to be, what behaviors you want to practice
- Are about you and only you
- Stated in the positive (exclude not, don't, didn't)
- The action is conscious, purposeful, committed
- The action makes you feel good, excited, jazzed, curious, empowered, inspired

Some examples might be:

I am willing to laugh and find humor whenever I feel stressed.

I am willing to nurture my body through exercise and a healthy diet.

I commit to exploring new career opportunities and trusting my intuition.

I intend to practice performing to the best of my ability at each tournament.

I am willing to release my expectations of others and be responsible for my choices.

I commit to complimenting my co-workers on their work.

I commit to trusting myself and releasing the judgments of others.

I choose to listen to my courageous inner voice and turn off my negative inner voice.

I am willing to take one risk in my career each day.

How many intentions should you write and how do you decide what is most important? While there may be several areas of your life that you would like to work on, I recommend focusing on 2-3 intentions at a time. Each intention requires commitment and practice. If you have too many, your focus will be too broad to master any one area. As you practice and old habits are replaced with new habits, you can begin to consider another area you would like to work on. Remember you are the common denominator in your life. You bring you with you wherever you go. If you live by your intentions, you will begin to notice changes in several areas of your life.

I recommend making both life intentions and situational intentions to my clients. For example, Mary had gained about twenty pounds over the last year. She was very self conscious of her weight gain. She was planning a trip to her hometown and was debating whether or not to contact several of her old friends to let them know when she was coming. She was considering traveling half way across the country and not seeing her dearest friends because of how she looked. She was worried about how self-conscious she would feel and about the possibility that her friends would secretly be judging her looks. Her internal dialogue and thoughts were creating her feelings of fear. As a coach, I asked her several questions about what she values and what impact her expectations were having on her. She decided that she valued seeing her friends more than worrying about feeling embarrassed. I asked her to create an inspiring intention about how she wanted to show up, how she wanted to participate in her life.

For her trip, her intention was:

I am willing to accept who I am today and share myself with the people I value most.

While she was on her trip and her feelings of being self-conscious about her weight came up, she repeated her intention. Accepting herself, as is, in the present, helped her focus on what she really valued--connecting with her dear friends. Her friends valued the person she is on the inside and surrounded her in love, without judgment of her size.

Values

How do you decide what intentions will be the most impactful? A good place to start is creating intentions that are in alignment with your personal value system. Make a list of priorities based on your personal values. Your values and your desires hold the key to creating your intentions.

Whatever we seek in others or in the world, we must first be willing to build in ourselves.

If you want love in your life, what are you willing to do? How can you show up in your life with the intention of being more loving to others? If you want people to be more understanding, what are you willing to do to ask for what you want or communicate more effectively? If you want more peace and less drama, how can you become more peaceful in your thoughts and actions? Again, you create your intentions based on your thoughts. Your intentions create your actions. Your actions create your reality. Living by intention also requires releasing disempowering expectations, taking personal responsibility, and following through with action. It is up to you and only you to start living by your intentions and commitments. You decide. It is your choice.

Action for Life Exercise

List what you value most. What are the top 5 things you value? Be specific. Here are some examples to get you started:

Career growth	Romance	Family
Health	Charity	Personal growth
Recreation	Spirituality	Friendship
Community	Personal space	Creativity
Fitness	Self care	Finances
Home	Travel	Environment

On a scale from 1-10, how satisfied are you in each of those top 5 categories?

How can you improve your satisfaction level? What action steps can you take?

Language

Language is extremely powerful. It is the verbalization of our thoughts and our beliefs. When you use empowering language, your outlook on life becomes more positive. When you use the language of intention, you are clearly stating to yourself and to the world that you are choosing the direction of your life. You are in charge of your present and your future. You choose to be the person you want to be. Language distinctly impacts your view of yourself and how the world perceives you. Again, you choose your thoughts and your language. When you are committed to taking responsibility and living with intention, your language will also shift. Eliminate disempowering language from your vocabulary.

Disempowering Language	Empowering Language
I can't	I can, I will
I should	I choose to
I compare myself	I value myself
Someday, I will	Today, I will
They think	I think
They feel	I feel
It is impossible	It is possible
I am trying	I am doing
I hope	I trust
I have to do it alone	I can request help
I regret	Next time, I will
There are problems	I see opportunities
I don't have the skills	I get to learn
Something always goes wrong	I see what is right

I hate	I prefer
This stinks	This challenges me
This is too hard	I can do this
I judge	I accept differences
You choose	I choose, I want
It is always something	I see an adventure
It is difficult	I am willing to work
But	And or Yet
It's up to you	I decide

The language of intention ties in personal responsibility with our commitments. When we start using the language of intention, we reclaim control over our lives.

Realizing that we have limitless choices enables us to have complete control over our responses to any circumstance. The power of choice gives us personal power. We get to decide to release expectations, to take responsibility for our lives, to evaluate choices, and to choose to live by our commitments. We get to create the life that we want to live.

Action for Life Exercise

What are the reasons you cannot move forward?

What are your excuses costing you?

How are your excuses benefiting you?

What does your inner wisdom tell you?

What do you want to change in your life?

What intention would support you?

What action steps would support you in living by this intention?

Action for Life Team

In what area of your life do you want to practice living by intention?

Who can you ask to support you in this area?

Chapter Strategy

There is always a choice. Stop acting on your emotions and start acting in alignment with your integrity, commitments, and highest values. Choose to live by intention.

Chapter 4 Key Points

- There is always a choice. Choices are limitless.

- The Law of Choices reveals that no matter what circumstances we face in life, we always have the ability to choose our direction. We have the power to remain stagnant or grow, live in fear or love, or to take action negatively or positively.

- The opposing forces in choice are the voice of fear versus the voice of inner wisdom (love).

- The Law of Integrity asks us to strive to know ourselves, live as ourselves, and act on our values. We betray ourselves when we do not act with integrity.

- Feelings are a temporary experience. They change as we change.

- The Principle of Intention is choosing to take action in alignment with your commitments and values, instead of your emotions.

- Excuses are feelings based, not fact based.

- Intentions require you to do something and move you toward a desired state of being.

- Turn excuses into intentions.

- Choose to use the language of intention.

Chapter 5

Embrace Unique. Embrace Your Authentic Self.

"What lies behind us and what lies before us are tiny matters compared to what lies within us."—Ralph Waldo Emerson

One day, when our boys were 5 and 6 years old, they were playing a game in the house and had accidentally broken a vase. In a game of chase, both boys had accidentally slid into a pedestal table, bumped the base, and knocked the vase off of the table. The vase landed on the floor and broke into hundreds of pieces. It seemed that both boys were equally responsible for the damage. Our older son began wailing and crying. Without even telling me, he ran to his room to give himself a time out while screaming at the top of his lungs that he was such a bad kid. Our other son felt bad as well, but his actions were very different. He came to me with some of the pieces, apologized, and asked what he could do to make it right.

I was aware that their personalities were very different, but I was fascinated by the differences in their actions. You may be thinking that their past experiences with me, their order of birth, or something else may have influenced their feelings. I am sure it did. Yet, the net result was, in that moment, each child responded in accordance with their own individual perceptions and beliefs. Without really being aware, each child made choices about how to handle the situation based upon their own internal dynamics. I saw my two sons experience the same set of circumstances and have totally different responses. One child seemed to let the situation roll off of his shoulders and the other child beat himself up endlessly. I wondered, "What do they believe about themselves? What do they believe about me? How did they learn to respond so differently?"

Self Concept

Our values, beliefs, and perceptions are intimately entwined. When we are born, we have a genetic predisposition to certain attributes, but our mind is essentially a blank slate. Our childhood environment influences our thoughts and perceptions because we pick up pieces of information from those around us, particularly our parents. It is a commonly held belief that we learn behaviors from modeling the behaviors of our parents and we learn to take in perspectives that become familiar to us. If we are brought up in a home that is filled with malevolence and criticism, we learn to view life with pessimism. If the attitudes and behaviors we witness are positive, we learn to view life with a more optimistic perspective. Our teachers, friends, and other role models also shape our beliefs. When we are young, naïve, and learning about the world, one small moment or one small interaction with another person may significantly impact how we feel about ourselves. If someone says that we are sensitive, we may take it in as fact. But, what does sensitive really mean? Does it mean that we are thoughtful and insightful? Or does it mean that we are overly emotional? What about my children who live in the same house, have the same genetics, and have the same parents to learn from? What caused them to respond differently to the same set of circumstances when the vase was broken? It seems that we start forming opinions of ourselves, our self concept, at a fairly young age. Everything we think we are, we are or we become.

Our genetics and our early childhood experiences play a role in our personalities. Yet, our beliefs about who we are and what is possible for us ultimately determine what we will become. We each choose, based on our belief system, how to respond in any and every situation. We learn to avoid perceived pain and to seek safety and/or pleasure. This happens both on a physical level and an emotional level. Two people may experience the same set of circumstances, but may respond in a totally different way to those circumstances because of their belief system.

Our self concept is the way we see ourselves. It is the culmination of thoughts, opinions, and beliefs about who we are and the qualities that we have. It is our definition of our value, whether we are lovable or not, what we are capable of, and how we perceive our purpose in the world. Our self concept is essentially a self evaluation of our qualities, attributes, strengths, and weaknesses. It is the perception of self, based upon both internal and external stimuli.

Our beliefs about ourselves shape how we interact in the world. How we interact in the world creates feedback and the feedback in turn, influences our self concept. In other words, if we interact with others using behaviors and language that are defensive and controlling, we receive feedback that is very different than if we were to engage in the world with positive and open behaviors. Our style of engaging in the world simply creates results. The beauty is that self concept can evolve as we evolve. Our thoughts can change and therefore, we can change. Our self concept is perception based. As our perceptions and behaviors shift, our self concept shifts.

Our core beliefs may remain constant, but as we grow, we may find that our perceptions about our capabilities and possibilities grow as well. For example, a person who is filled with self-doubt will have a very different self concept than someone who has self-confidence. As we have already learned, self-confidence is built by taking risks and stepping out of our comfort zone. When we take risks, self-doubt starts to melt away and self-confidence grows. As our self-confidence grows, our self concept also changes and evolves.

The other thing that I find interesting about self concept is that it is not always accurate because it is perception based, not necessarily fact based. Our perceptions are limited by the knowledge we have at any given moment. An analogy might be looking at a forest from different views. When we walk into a forest, our view is that of the details of the trees, leaves, stones and sky within our view at ground level. If we were to climb to the top of a hill and look at that same spot in the forest, our viewpoint would be a viewpoint from above. The trees, leaves, stones, and sky would still be exactly the same, but what we see would look completely different. The forest did not change; only our viewpoint and perceptions changed.

Perceptions can lead us to see things in different ways depending upon our viewpoint. As we are willing to see the trees differently, we must be willing to see ourselves differently. We must realize that we have limits on our perspective and we must be willing to look beyond those limitations at any given moment. Who we are is a result of how we choose to think and how we choose to show up in the world. We are influenced by the experiences in our lives. Yet, we always have a choice about what beliefs we choose to internalize and what beliefs we choose to reject. Our lives are a process of evolving, changing, and growing.

> *We have limits on our perspective at any given moment. We must commit to seeing beyond those limitations.*

The Law of Compassion

The Law of Compassion invites us to be compassionate as we move through our personal evolution. It asks us to have compassion for ourselves and others because as we move through the journey of life, we are all just doing the best that we can with the knowledge and skills we have at any given moment. We each have a belief system that sets into motion our thoughts, attitudes, and actions. You have probably heard the phrase, "When we know better, we do better." As we begin to grow, trust ourselves more, and access our own inner wisdom instead of listening to the voice of fear, we can begin to make more enlightened choices in our lives. So, the Law of Compassion guides us to act from a place of understanding and compassion, no matter where we each are on our path.

Compassion must begin within us. We cannot have compassion for others, until we are willing to have it for ourselves. Compassion is the understanding that we are in the process of learning, of growing, and of changing. We do not have all of the answers and we will have lapses in judgment. We will have moments where we wished that we had made a different choice, but through compassion we learn to embrace our humanity. We learn forgiveness. We learn the power of choice. We learn that we can make different choices next time. The Law of Compassion invites us to see life from a viewpoint of connection to our humanity, rather than judgment, anger, or ignorance. It guides us to forgive ourselves and to understand that we are humans with human frailties. When we have compassion for ourselves, we can turn off our self-critical voice and turn on our self-loving voice. We can stop judging ourselves and embrace the idea that we are on a journey of growth.

Compassion does not give us an excuse to act inappropriately when we know better or to allow others to walk on us, but to free ourselves from our limited perceptions. Since we all have fear, we are all capable of acting out in ways that do not serve our highest potential. Compassion gives us permission to increase our awareness of fearful thinking instead of beating ourselves up through self-criticism. It also gives us greater insight into others.

Just as we can act out inappropriately because of fear based thinking, others can as well. Realizing that other people had the same fears as me was a significant revelation in my life. There were times when I just could not understand why people acted the way they did and I took it personally. I found their choices to be very hurtful. I was willing to look at myself and notice how my behaviors contributed to my feelings. Yet, when I realized that fear was driving their behavior, I was able to detach and stop taking it personally. It was not about me. It was their fear and their self-loathing that caused them to act out. I found compassion because I imagined that living in constant, perpetual, overwhelming fear is like living in an emotional prison.

You will come across people in life that you want to stay away from because of the choices that they make. Some people are emotionally damaging to us. They may lash out in fear. They may be constant victims who revel in their misery and drain us of our energy. There may be people that you love dearly, but seem to see the negative side of everything and it feels exhausting to be around them. We can choose to have compassion for people consumed by their fear or who act out, without succumbing to our own fear or behaving the way that they do. We can have compassion while enforcing boundaries.

Boundaries are personal standards of acceptable and non-acceptable behavior. Boundaries are limits that define what behaviors we are willing to accept and not willing to accept from others. When we set boundaries, they are consistent for all people that we come in contact with, not just certain individuals. We can enforce the boundaries that we value while still choosing to be compassionate with the humanity and imperfections of others. In many ways, compassion is a gift to ourselves because it helps keep us focused on our responsibilities, intentions, and ability to make choices.

Here are the main components to compassion:

1. We cannot have compassion for others until we have compassion for ourselves. Compassion is turning off our self-critical voice and turning on our self-loving voice.

2. Compassion is seeing that we all are in a process of growth and evolution.

3. We are all limited by the knowledge we have in the present moment. We cannot teach or give what we do not have; therefore, compassion is the understanding that ignorance or lack of knowledge influences behavior.

4. Compassion is the understanding that we all have fears and sometimes fear can motivate undesirable behaviors.

5. Judgment and compassion cannot exist together. Judgment blocks growth.

6. Realize that at any given moment, our perceptions are limited by our current viewpoint. Compassion is the understanding that our perceptions have limitations.

7. We can be compassionate while still enforcing boundaries. We can decide what behaviors we are willing to accept from others and what behaviors we are not willing to accept. We can choose to enforce minimum standards while still seeing the humanity in others through compassion.

8. Compassion and forgiveness are synergistic.

Compassion is critically important to our overall happiness, self-esteem, and our ability to live our best life. So many of us have no awareness of how little compassion we have, especially for ourselves, and how we sabotage our ability to live an authentic life. Let's talk about some of the most common ways we undermine ourselves.

The Self-Critical Voice

Fear wants us to stay safe inside our comfort zone. Our self-critical voice is the voice of fear. They are one in the same. The voice of fear wants to keep you emotionally safe and protect you from pain, from hurt, from being wounded. It does not want you to take risks and venture outside of your comfort zone because you will feel vulnerable. It is the voice that tells you that you will look foolish, that you will fail, and that you are not good enough. The voice of fear does not know what your possibilities are and it does not care. It is trying to protect you, to stop you from expanding and growing. Fear does not want you to take risks, try new things, or reach for your potential because there is the chance you may experience discomfort, hurt or pain. Fear calls attention to every perceived mistake or imperfection to prove to you that you should stay exactly where you are. It judges you without compassion. It keeps a record of all of your failures, but not once reminds you of your accomplishments or strengths. It blames and finds fault. It keeps you seeking validation from external sources instead of trusting your own inner wisdom.

Often, we do not realize that it is the voice of fear talking. We say random little negative things to ourselves and we think nothing of it. We use negative labels and self-criticism far more often than any of us realize. Yet, each and every time we participate in negative self-talk, our thoughts are creating our reality. We are telling ourselves that we are limited, unworthy, or undeserving of happiness, passion, and abundance. What does your critical voice say to you?

Here are some common examples of a Self-Critical Voice:

Nothing ever works out for me.
I can't seem to do anything right.
My life is a mess.
What is wrong with me?
Everyone, but me, can do this.
I can't win.
Maybe I'm just lazy.
I must be incompetent.
I have wasted another day.
I must be unlovable.
I am not good enough.
I don't do enough.
I should have known better.
I should be more organized.
I am just not good at that.
I can never seem to focus.
I don't deserve happiness.
I am so clumsy...
Every time I try, I give up.
Today just isn't my day.
I am a failure.
Sometimes, I just hate myself.

I am a disappointment.
I let people down.
I let myself down.
My feelings just don't count.
I don't matter.
I don't trust myself.
I am a fool.
I am not good with money.
I am not good with words.
I am not good in relationships.
I mess everything up.
I am not as qualified as the rest.
I am not as smart as the others.
I am a loser.
How can I be so stupid?
I am impatient.
I am always late.
Nobody understands me.
If only I had better skills.
If only I were more intelligent.
I am not creative.
I am so unlucky.

No Judgment

The examples above are examples of self-criticism and self-criticism carries judgment. Judgment is a feeling based perception, not a fact based thought. If we are compassionate with ourselves and others, then judgment cannot exist.

Without judgment, we would see ourselves as moving through life in a process of growing from our challenges, experiences, and opportunities. Similarly, we would see others moving through that same process, even though they might be at a different place than us in their personal journey. The Law of Compassion releases expectations and judgments and asks us to understand that each of us is simply doing the best we can within the boundaries of our current knowledge and skills.

Compassion and judgment cannot occupy our thoughts at the same time. When we judge ourselves or others, we are creating resistance to our own evolution and keeping ourselves stuck in patterns of limited thinking. We judge by setting expectations of the ideal, the ideal way to act, the ideal outcome, or the ideal life. Once again, we are setting ourselves up for disappointment because we do not live in an ideal world. We live in a world where people are growing, learning, changing, and evolving. There is no state of perfection, a place that we get to when we do everything right. Judging ourselves or anyone else against the ideal keeps us stuck in our fears because we are setting a bar that can never be reached. Judgment keeps us stuck in our emotional perceptions instead of seeing the facts.

Emotional Distortions

We learn from a young age to process our experiences through a mental filter. Our filter is really a perception, a way of processing information that is personal to each one of us. It is a way of sorting information that is in alignment with our belief systems. As with my sons, a statement like, "Oh, the vase is broken." is interpreted by each child through their own filter or perception. One son might see that statement as a neutral statement of fact and the other son might see it as an accusation that he broke the vase and is a bad kid. The same statement is taken in and processed to have different meaning based upon each boy's perceptions. When we push information through our filters and interpret the meaning in accordance with our personal perceptions, we are often distorting the information depending on our emotional state. We may not necessarily be hearing it in the way it was spoken or intended. We are hearing it in a way that matches our beliefs. These are emotional distortions of information. Filtering is just one way our emotions and perceptions distort information.

When we use words such as *always, every, everyone, none, no one, never*, or any other word that makes a broad generalization, we are often distorting information and internalizing a perception. We are distorting the facts. This usually happens when we attach negative feelings to a particular experience. Then, as we go forward in life, we generalize or attach the same meaning to all future experiences.

For example, if we feel that someone at work does not like us, we then begin to generalize and feel that *everyone* at work does not like us. The language might be: "Nothing ever works out for me." "No one ever likes me." "I am always the loser." When we use these generalizations, not only are we distorting the truth, we are disempowering ourselves through our misrepresentations of the facts. As a Coach, I interrupt my clients when they make these generalizations. I ask, "Is it really true that no one in your entire office building likes you? Not one single person? Has each and every person said this to you?" Of course, it is not true. Attaching broad generalizations to your thinking, keeps you from living in reality and it diminishes your self-esteem. Get these words out or your vocabulary and out of your thinking.

Sometimes we get stuck in labeling ourselves or others. Labels are closely related to generalizations, but they focus on grouping people by perceived traits rather than noticing the uniqueness of individuals. It is a way of sorting people into groups in order to give them a place to belong in our minds--and it is also a judgment. People do not fit into molds when we are willing to see each person as an individual. In high school, we might have divided people into clicks: the Geeks, the Jocks, the Surfers, the Rockers, etc., but in reality, people are multi-dimensional and do not fit into cookie cutter categories. We also label ourselves by making generalizations such as: fat, slow, clumsy, lazy…The problem with labels is they separate us from others and diminish our self-esteem by limiting our thinking.

We also make distortions when we make assumptions about what we believe other people are thinking. We act as if we can read their minds and know their thoughts. For instance, Jenna spent a great deal of time and energy in making assumptions about what other people were thinking. When she was feeling insecure, she was sure the rest of the world could see her low self-esteem. She expected perfection out of her performance at work. When she did not perform to her own high standards, she was sure her boss was disappointed in her, too. The most damaging part of this type of emotional distortion is that Jenna began to act as if her boss was disappointed in her performance. Her perceptions were not based in reality. She had received no such feedback from her boss. Still, she worked long hours, second-guessed herself, and became exhausted trying to please her boss. She was on the verge of resigning because she believed that she just could not do a good enough job.

The truth was that her boss was not at all disappointed in her performance. From the time she was hired, he was very pleased. She assumed that she could read his mind, his body language, and his facial expressions. She would say things like, "I can tell by the look on his face." Or "I just know." Jenna was forming conclusions based on her perceptions, not the facts.

Ask yourself:

Are my perceptions the truth or am I making them up?

What *facts* do I really know in this situation?

We also make emotional distortions when we personalize information or events and somehow make everything that happens in the world directly related to ourselves. We make assumptions that the words or events that happen around us are directly related to us personally. This happened in my own life. My husband made a statement that the kitchen is messy and I interpreted it to mean that he was complaining about my housekeeping skills. Yet, that was not what he said. In that moment, I assumed that his comment was somehow aimed at me and I immediately got defensive. My filter told me that he was taking a pot shot at me. I made it personal based upon my own judgments of myself and the fact that I thought I should have already cleaned the kitchen. In reality, he had just made an observation and was willing to step in and help.

These are the types of misunderstandings that destroy relationships. When we assume, we are making things up. When we personalize information or events as if they are directly related to us, we are giving ourselves way too much importance. Not everything that happens around us is related *to* us. We are not the center of everyone else's thoughts. We just are not! When we think we are, we are distorting the facts. Just as we let go of disempowering expectations, we must let go of our assumptions and emotional distortions. We must choose to separate fact and fiction.

Rejection

No one likes the feeling of rejection. It feels like we do not belong, do not fit in, or are unwanted. There are many ways that rejection shows up in our lives and there are many behaviors associated with feeling rejected. The bottom line is rejection brings up feelings of being unworthy or inadequate. To make matters worse, when we are in the midst of being rejected by someone else, we have absolutely no control over the outcome and we feel powerless. They are deciding the result, not us. We can try asking for clarity, rephrasing, redirecting, or repositioning, but ultimately, they decide to accept or reject. With rejection, we are completely at the mercy of someone else. Or are we?

My eleven year old son came home from school, recently, armed with intense enthusiasm to sell magazine subscriptions for a school fund raiser. The school recommended that the kids not solicit door to door, but through e-mail. My son sat down in front of the computer for hours and e-mailed a personal note to everyone he could think of, from the orthodontist to family and friends. Days passed and he only received a few responses. He was disappointed and let me know that he was going to stop trying to win any of the sales contests. When I asked him why, he said that he felt rejected and he did not want to experience more rejection. I asked him to explain further and tell me the feelings that he was experiencing. He said that he felt a little bit ignored because very few people responded; he felt bad about himself because he felt like he did not do a good enough job promoting the magazines in his personal note to each recipient; and he felt inferior to the other kids who were selling more magazines than he was. He was feeling helpless, inadequate and very down on himself.

I told my son, "Reject rejection." To which he responded, "Huh? Mom, speak English." I asked, "How do you know that you did not do a good job in your personal note? What are the reasons you feel like the rejection was personal? What were you expecting? How do you know how many people actually checked their e-mail? How do you know how many magazines the other kids sold on their first try?"

We sat down and talked about all of the assumptions, generalizations, and personalization's he had made. We talked about how he was creating the belief that he would experience more rejection if he continued to try. When he started, he had zero sales and now he had three sales. He was not worse off than when he started, he was actually ahead. Even if he had zero sales, he still would not have lost anything for trying. The only way he could lose anything is through rejecting himself. He was starting to feel better, but was still having difficulty detaching from his feelings. He said, "I failed to sell magazines, so I must not be good at that." He was still personalizing the rejection instead of considering alternate paths or solutions. He was internalizing his feelings, labeling himself as a poor salesman, and staying stuck in rejection.

I decided to try another example: asking a girl to a school dance. I inquired, "How would you feel if she said no?" He laughed and said, "Rejected." "What else?" I asked. He said, "Like a loser, unwanted, foolish, and embarrassed. I would probably feel like there was something undesirable about me." Again, we went through his list of assumptions, labels, and personalization's. I said, "What if her parents don't allow her to go to dances and she was embarrassed to tell you? What if she does not know how to dance and that is why she said no? What if she is going to be out of town that weekend? Is she rejecting you or are *you* rejecting you by assuming that because she said no, there is something wrong with you? Rejection can only happen when we reject ourselves." He grinned from ear to ear and said, "Mom, this is so cool! I love it when you break it down like this. I was making up stuff in my mind and I was rejecting myself." He gave me a huge bear hug. I knew he got it.

We only truly feel rejected when we reject ourselves, our worth, our opinions, and our values. When we feel rejected, the feelings are coming from within, not from any external source. The act of rejecting is simply saying that there is not a "fit". It does not mean that you as a person are rejected, unworthy, or inadequate. It simply means that the pieces do not fit together at this time or under these circumstances. Picture a puzzle. The pieces fit where they fit. We would not expect a square peg to fit in a round hole. There is nothing inferior about the square peg; it would just fit better in a square hole. If you are a manager and are interviewing candidates, not every candidate will get hired. You are choosing to hire the person with the best "fit" for the job. The other candidates may be highly talented and qualified, but only one can get the job and you choose the one with the best fit.

> *The feeling of rejection is a result of choosing to reject ourselves. It is rejecting our own opinions, needs, and worth.*

When someone does not agree with your political views, they are not rejecting you as a person; they are rejecting your views. They are disagreeing with you and you are disagreeing with them. It is not personal. We all have criteria that we place value on in order to find the right fit with our beliefs, needs, and wants. We all have choices. If you were ending a relationship with someone else and took all of the emotions out of the equation, the bottom line would be that the relationship was not a fit with your needs at this time in your life. That's all.

Rejection is not about being rejected by others; rejection can only happen when we reject ourselves. When there is not a fit and we take it personally, we are rejecting ourselves. When we internalize feelings of unworthiness or inadequacy, we are rejecting ourselves. When we allow our self concept to be lessened because there is not a fit, we are rejecting ourselves. Rejecting ourselves is letting fear run our life. It is rejecting what we know to be true and interpreting a differing opinion as having more validity. When my son came home with such enthusiasm to sell magazines, he believed in himself. He believed in his abilities and his worth. When he felt rejected, he allowed the rejection to diminish his beliefs. He rejected himself instead of considering other options.

I want to share with you a story about a wise elder. The wise elder was a calm and centered man. He lived a peaceful, serene life. One day a stranger, who had heard the stories about the elder, decided to challenge the elder's peacefulness. The stranger started to scream at the elder. He ranted and raved. He called the elder names and belittled him. He challenged the elder's character and did everything he could think of to get a reaction from the old man. Finally, as the stranger started to run out of energy, the wise elder spoke. He asked the stranger a question, "If I am given a gift and I choose not to accept it, to whom does the gift belong?" The stranger answered that the gift would still belong to the gift giver. The wise elder smiled and said, "Yes, I agree. I choose not to accept your rage, venom, or opinions. They are yours to keep."

The elder made the choice not to entertain the stranger's opinions. He did not feel rejected or inadequate. He did not get defensive or reactive. He did not take in the stranger's poison or venomous words. He believed that the words were a reflection of the person speaking them, not of himself. He knew his truth. No matter what the stranger said, he did not reject himself.

Trust that you know your truth. When others reject you, they are saying that it is not a fit. When others are demeaning, it is a reflection of their own negative perceptions at work. So, we have the choice to align our thinking with feeling unworthy or reject it as false. When we accept that person's opinion over our truth, we reject ourselves and give our power away. Unknowingly, we are allowing someone else to run our life. We are setting ourselves up to devalue our own feelings of worth and self-esteem.

Like any other negative emotion, feeling rejected is a call to action. When we feel rejected, we have choices. We can view the situation from another perspective. Remember, the appearance of the forest is vastly different when we change viewpoints. Depending on the situation, we can investigate alternate actions. We can take the experience in as an opportunity to learn about ourselves and others. We can have compassion for ourselves. We can get clear on what our needs and values are and seek to find the fit that is right for us. We can stand tall in our personal truth.

The feeling of rejection is an opportunity to evaluate your thoughts, feelings, and actions while you were engaged in the situation. If you need to make changes, be willing to make them. Take responsibility for your choices and actions. Learn from the experience. Be willing to invest in yourself and learn new skills. But, do not reject yourself. Do not tell yourself that you are not worthy of love, happiness, or success. Remember, rejection only happens when we reject ourselves.

If you read my story in the beginning of this book, you know that I had a strong fear of rejection. I liked it when people counted on me because I felt valued. I valued being needed more than I valued my own needs and as a result, I made myself physically ill. The funny thing was that I did not see myself as someone whose life was run by fear. I really believed that I was fearless. Until, of course, I ended up sick in bed with lots of time to think about how I got there. I learned a great deal about the fear of rejection and how it shows up in subtle ways. I want to share with you some of the signs that *fear of rejection* is impacting your choices. Here are some signs that reveal when you are rejecting yourself.

Signs that you are rejecting yourself:

Focusing on external opinions instead of your own... feeling hypersensitive to feedback... people pleasing... overexplaining... justifying... compromising your own needs... making others feel ok at your expense...detaching from your own needs... adapting your opinions to feel accepted... sugar coating the truth to avoid disapproval... avoiding speaking up when your really want to... feeling anxious when others disagree with you... being overly independent to avoid needing others... judging and comparing your work... feeling your creativity or talent is inferior... sacrificing taking care of yourself in order to take care of others... focusing on achievement or doing in an effort to have value... avoiding appearing vulnerable... avoiding participating fully in life... standing on the side lines and allowing life to pass you by... internalizing rejection and devaluing yourself.

We must be willing to risk facing the feelings of rejection in order to grow. If we are not willing to take that risk, we will never know what we are capable of. If we seek to avoid rejection, we also seek to avoid success and we do not live authentic lives. If we avoid risking rejection, we avoid embracing our lives and all that is possible for us. In order to break free of the fear of rejection, we must fully embrace who we are. We must value our own needs and opinions and learn not to take things personally. Rejection is a part of life, but we can choose not to reject ourselves.

Forgiveness

If we are going to move forward in our lives and create the life that we want to live, we must leave the past behind us. In order to truly put the past behind us, we must be willing to forgive ourselves and others. The Law of Compassion asks us to be gentle because we are all just doing the best that we can with the tools and knowledge we have at any given moment. Forgiveness is learning from our experiences, but accepting that the past is over. There is no way to go back in time and change events. When we forgive, we are accepting the truth of what happened instead of what we think should have happened or what we wanted to happen. It is letting go of "if only" thinking and it is letting go of blame. Forgiveness is surrendering to the reality of the event, not blocking it, stuffing your feelings down, or replaying the event over and over in your mind. If we are focused on the past, we cannot fully live in the present moment. Being willing to forgive is being willing to give yourself the gift of inner peace and healing. Forgiveness is really a gift to yourself, not anyone else. Compassion and forgiveness are synergistic: together they can give us the freedom to live our best life.

Forgiveness does not mean that you agree with what happened or condone the inappropriate behavior of someone else. People act out in fear. People who do not love themselves often find it difficult to act in a loving way. People can only do what they know how to do. Some of my clients have lingering anger at their parents. In a perfect world, parents would do all of the right things. Unfortunately, when they do not have the appropriate skills or knowledge, they can make poor choices. They cannot teach self-love if they do not know self-love. They cannot give what they do not have.

Our voice of fear tells us to build evidence to validate our feelings and place blame on others for the status of our lives. Forgiveness is not agreement; it is letting go of your need to prove your position, your need to be right, or your desire to do it over again. It is not a competition with a winner and a loser. This is your life!

Forgiveness is embracing humanity in yourself and in others, so that you can be free of the past. If you really think about it, holding on to anger, hurt, or wounds takes a great deal of energy. Do not give your energy to another person or situation from the past. Forgiveness does not mean that you choose to forget; but that you choose compassion and you choose to expend your energy elsewhere.

Maybe you do not agree with your own past behavior. Maybe you have made choices that were hurtful or fear based. Sometimes, even when we have the tools, the voice of fear drives our thinking and we say or do things we later regret. Fear drives us to be defensive, judgmental, and reactive. We must remember that forgiveness is a gift to ourselves. Holding on to shame, guilt, and hurt keeps us stuck in our negative feelings and pushes us farther and farther away from our authentic self. Take responsibility for your life and for your choices—and then forgive the past.

When we hold on to trying to protect ourselves from being hurt or being vulnerable, we are not living as our true self. We are choosing to let the voice of fear call the shots and when we are living in fear, we cannot access true compassion. I have found that forgiveness is a process. It is not a one time event, but a commitment to intention. Depending on the situation, it can be a very long process. No matter how much time it takes, forgiveness and compassion are critical skills to develop in order to move forward to a fulfilling life. I have found with my clients and in my own life that there are three important steps in forgiveness.

Steps for forgiveness:

1) Acknowledge your feelings. Utilize a non-destructive way of releasing your feelings. Find a place where you can be with yourself. Cry. Vent. Yell. Let it out. Write all of your feelings down on a piece of paper and hold nothing back. Let your feelings be what they are and let them flow out of you. Write about what made you angry; what hurt you; what scared you; what you needed and did not get; what made you sad; and any other underlying feelings. Be as honest as you possibly can.

2) Take responsibility for everything you did or did not do. Taking responsibility is not blaming or fault finding. It is simple acknowledgment of the facts. If you wanted to speak up and did not, take responsibility. If you said inappropriate things, take responsibility. If you did not put effort in or were emotionally checked out, take responsibility. If you had even one moment where you were nasty, mean, or cold, take responsibility. If you are holding responsibility that does not belong to you, take responsibility for letting it go.

The only exception to this point is children who are victims of circumstances outside of their control. Children are not responsible for choices of adults.

3) Look for gifts. Find gratitude for what you learned, gained, or developed as a result of the experience. How did your character grow? What skills did you develop? There are gifts in every experience if you are willing to see them. When you are able to shift your thinking from the hurt you feel to gratitude for the strength you gained, your feelings will begin to shift and move toward healing.

Changing Perspectives Facilitates Forgiveness

I went through my own journey of forgiveness. It was a unique family situation and for many years, I did not even realize how hurt I was or how angry I was with my brother. We had never been terribly close and I admit I felt rejected by him from the time we were very young. My parents called it sibling rivalry, but to me, it felt like more than that. I wanted his praise and approval. I wanted my big brother to like me and to be proud of me. Because we were less than two years apart and he was my only sibling, I wanted to hang out with him, but it seemed that he did not want to hang out with me. When he acted cold, mean, or lashed out at me, I internalized the feelings and felt worthless. When I wanted to speak up, I felt pressured to let it go and look the other way.

As adults, there was a precipitating event and the pain cut through me like a knife. I told myself all of the things I should do, like let it go once again, but this time was different. I was flooded with feelings—feelings from the present and unresolved feelings from the past. The emotional wound felt very raw and I just kept wondering how he could do this to me. I felt victimized. I asked him to change his position or at least consider mine, but he was sure that he was right. I did not really see a right or wrong, I could only see that he did not care about my feelings once again. I made the very difficult decision to sever what little relationship we had left.

Of course, I heard lots of "how could you do that, he is your brother, your blood." I just knew that I had to take care of myself, somehow, someway, and my relationship with him drained me emotionally. As I started to work through my feelings, I wrote many, many letters. Most of them got thrown away, but I did mail one of them. I think I was hoping that the feelings I had been carrying all of those years would finally be heard. Of course, my letter did not change anything. In retrospect, it probably made things worse because it kept his defenses up. The more my family pressured me and told me what I should do, the more my anger grew. Forgiveness does not work when we are doing it for someone else.

After some time, I decided to look at the situation from a different perspective, a perspective of invincible self-esteem and self-worth. If, in fact, I had not desired validation from him throughout our childhood, how would the events feel to me now? If I looked at our relationship from a place of complete self-trust and self-confidence, would his actions wound me in the same way? I envisioned myself standing tall feeling secure and self-confident. I envisioned myself filled with invincible self-trust and worth, with no need for validation. Then, I envisioned the same events that I thought were so painful happening again. It hit me. If my perspective had been different, I would not have felt the same way. I realized that my feelings would have been very different. I realized that even though I thought his behaviors were inappropriate and crossed boundaries, *I* had made the choice to reject myself and take in those negative feelings for all those years. *I* had made the choice to expect him to be different than he really was. *I* had made the choice to look the other way and hold my feelings in. *I* had made the choice to give my power away. While I did not agree with his actions, it was the feelings within *me* that were so damaging to my self-esteem.

I took responsibility for all of those years of letting it go and looking the other way. I took responsibility for being too nice and too forgiving in my early years when I knew that I really wanted to change the direction of our relationship. I took responsibility for accepting how he treated me and for not enforcing my own boundaries. I took responsibility for not standing up for myself and for allowing myself to feel powerless for so long. I took responsibility for expecting him to be different than he really was. I took responsibility for my anger and for severing our relationship. Then, I gave myself lots and lots of compassion because I am a human being in the process of learning and at the time, I did not have the skills to do anything else. I forgave myself and I forgave him.

When my brother and I re-connected, I told him honestly how I felt. He really had no concept of what was going on within me. He said that he never wanted me to feel that way and acknowledged that his own fears and self-doubts had kept him in his own emotional jail. I felt deep compassion for both of us. Today, our relationship is stronger than it has ever been and I am grateful for the experience. I learned so much about myself, about rejection, about compassion, and about forgiveness. I was reminded once again that personal responsibility is critically important in living my life to the fullest. I would not be the person I am today without that experience. Even if he and I were not able to re-build a relationship, the gifts of learning about myself will always be mine.

Self-Worth

We have already talked about how our self concept can change as our perceptions change, but worth does not change. Worth is constant and infinite. It can never be taken away, lost, or diminished. No matter what you experience in your life, you are born with worth and it remains constant. Worth cannot and does not ever increase or decrease. So many of us hear our negative voice of fear telling us we just are not good enough or that we are unworthy. Yet, this is not possible because we are each born with worth and worth does not change. We may feel unworthy, but that is a perception, not a fact. You may lose your job, but your worth does not change. You may get divorced, but your worth does not change. You may make an inappropriate choice; live in fear; or not fit in with society, but your worth does not change. You do not have to meet certain criteria to have worth. You already have it.

Many of us define our worth by what we do, not who we are. We equate worth with "doing" and "achieving". I know I did. When I became sick and could no longer "do", my self-worth seemed to just evaporate. I felt worthless if I could not accomplish something. So many of us evaluate ourselves by how many tasks we can complete in a day or how many activities we do with our children. We evaluate ourselves by the achievement of goals; weight lost or gained, salaries, occupations, and looks.

We see a ship captain as having value where there are ships and water and a stock broker as having value on Wall Street. However, if the ship captain and the stock broker find themselves on top of the Andes Mountains, they may not be perceived as offering as much value. In reality, their circumstances changed, but their worth as human beings did not. We must realize that worth is a concept that we arbitrarily decide to attach meaning to through our perceptions. Worth is not based on what we own, what we do, or how we look. Worth is in each one of us equally and wholly. A surgeon does not have more worth than a janitor. A tall model does not have more worth than someone short in stature. We all have gifts to share with the world and our gifts all have value.

> *We create a vision in our mind that all of these people, that we don't even know or like, are somehow evaluating whether or not we are good enough. We must remember that our immeasurable worth is constant and ever present.*

In the past, I would attach the word "enough" to my worth. I was not outgoing enough. I was not a good enough writer. I was not tall enough. Enough for whom? Who were all of these people who I imagined were secretly evaluating me? It was all in my head. Whenever we cannot feel our worth, our perceptions and fears are tainting our thinking because worth is ever present. Worth is not determined by how you measure up or any outside factor. When we decide that worth is constant, we can let go of the perceptions that keep us feeling like we are not enough. We no longer feel the need to compare ourselves with others or stand in judgment. In order to feel our worth, we must change our self-critical dialogue to a self-loving dialogue.

I have altered the statements from the "Self-Critical Voice" section to reflect a "Self-Loving Voice."

Things work out for me.
I do all kinds of things right.
My life is a wondrous journey.
What is right with me?
I can do this.
I can win.
I'm productive.
I am competent.
I have utilized another day.
I am lovable.
I am good enough.
I do enough.
I trust myself.
I am organized.
I am good at that.
I can seem to focus.
I desire happiness.
I am so agile.
Every time I try, I learn.
Today just is my day.
I am a winner.
Sometimes, I just love myself.
I am a delight.

I lift people up.
I lift myself up.
My feelings do count.
I do matter.
I do trust myself.
I am wise.
I am good with money.
I am good with words.
I am good in relationships.
I contribute.
I have many skills.
I am as smart as the others.
I am a winner.
I am so smart.
I am patient.
I am on time.
People understand me.
I have great customers.
I am intelligent.
I am creative.
I am so lucky.
I have enough time.
I am youthful and exuberant.

How could your life change if you talked to yourself in a positive way? How would it feel to go through your day affirming all of your worth and your brilliant qualities? Imagine how your self-satisfaction and self-esteem would flourish. Imagine embracing all of who you are, your authentic self.

Authentic Self

Your authentic self is the real you. It is the true you without all of roles we play in our life. Your authentic self is the culmination of all of your gifts, talents, insights, intuition, abilities, and interests. Your authentic self is the "you" that you were born to be. It is the "you" that you were before you experienced pain, fear, or started putting up protective emotional barriers. There is no one else like you and only you were born to fulfill your purpose. When we live as our authentic self, our feelings of fear and powerlessness melt away.

When we believe that fear is speaking the truth, it takes courage to challenge our beliefs. It takes courage to tell your voice of fear that it is not real. It is not who you are. The voice of fear is not the voice of your true self. Your true self is the voice of your inner wisdom, intuition, and self-love. Remember, we are fully responsible for every aspect of our lives including the way we talk to ourselves. Thank your fear for wanting to keep you safe and then take control of your internal guidance system—your thoughts. Think a new thought and take a new action. Tell fear that you appreciate the warning, but that you can handle anything that comes your way. Learn how to hear your voice of inner wisdom.

One of my clients once asked me how she could tell if the voice in her head was the voice of fear or the voice of her inner wisdom. The voice of fear wants to keep you where you are, safe in your comfort zone. It will condemn, criticize, or judge to keep you there because it does not want you to risk experiencing pain or discomfort. It is kind of like a dysfunctional parent that is overly protective and overly afraid for your safety. It says, "Don't fall; you will look foolish. You are not qualified to try something new; you will fail."

Conversely, the voice of your authentic self is filled with self-love. It does not judge or condemn. It wants you to take down your walls of protection and show the world the amazing, unique person that you are. Your authentic self wants you to risk, grow, learn, and strive for your best life. It encourages you to be yourself, to honor yourself, and to have compassion for yourself. You authentic self knows that you are capable of great things. It knows that you are unique, that there is no one just like you. Your authentic self is your natural state of being. It is the state that you were born to be: complete, healthy, whole, and surrounded in love.

To live authentically, we must decide that only we define who we are. The outside world does not know us the way we know ourselves. We are not defined by our childhood or our parents. We are not defined by the people who judged us. We are not defined by our surroundings or our fears. Those things are separate from who we are as individuals. We decide who we are. We determine what we think, what we do, and how we feel.

In every one of us, there is a unique, distinct individual that has the power to shine like the sun. When we live authentically, we are living for ourselves and deciding with intention how we spend our time. We leave the past behind, anticipate joy in the future, and live completely in the present moment. We live in chosen roles, not roles assigned to us by someone else. We know our likes and dislikes. We follow our heart's desire and pursue interests that we feel passionate about. We wake up looking forward to the adventures of the day and go to sleep feeling satisfied. When a challenge arises, we look within ourselves to find the answers. We know our personal truth, what we need to change and what we need to keep. We do not waste our time focusing on controlling the external or giving our power to someone else. We feel centered, inspired, and peaceful because we know that we are in charge of our choices and our lives.

When we live as our authentic self, we gain more energy. We can slow down and listen to our voice of inner wisdom instead of running on the hamster wheel of life. Our inner wisdom or intuition guides us to live as our true self. Yet, when we live listening to our voice of fear or live controlled by expectations, we cannot hear our intuition. It takes a great deal of energy to live as someone you are not and when you decide to be you, you will feel energized.

Our outer world is always a reflection of our inner world. Our outer circumstances reflect our inner thoughts and feelings. When our inner world is congruent with our authentic self, our life really works. We feel a peacefulness, satisfaction, and serenity. The struggle with the outside world ends and we start to really live. It is our responsibility to focus on being who we are. The happiest people are people who feel a sense of significance and contribution to the world. There is no greater gift to give or contribution to make than just being you.

> *To live authentically, we must decide that only we define who we are.*

Sometimes we get so caught up in the responsibilities of life that we lose ourselves and we do not know how to find our authentic self. Re-discovering all of the things you love is the first step. What lights you up? What do you feel passionate about? What did you love to do in your childhood? What were your favorite subjects in school? What part of yourself have you given up because life became too demanding? Look over the following list and see if you feel excited about any of the following things. This list is meant to inspire you, so please feel free to add your own.

Belly laugh just because	Mentor kids
Connect with nature	Write a story
Experience a new culture	Create something
Challenge your brain to learn	Physical exercise
Read	Take lessons

Listen to music	Climb and hike
Play music	Ballroom Dancing
Volunteer your time	Help others
Travel	Meditate
Play with your kids	Make time for friends
Get organized	Build with your hands
Embark on a new career	Open a business
Improve body image	Share your love
Share your expertise	Spend time with family
Try a new hobby	Learn to fly
Relocate	Go to school

For me, I have always known that I enjoy helping others look at their lives and emotions in a different way. I have been a self-help book junky ever since I could read. I knew I had great intuition and a way of understanding others. Despite having been told that I should look into writing as a career, I did not identify myself as a writer. The fear response of comparing myself to other writers, who were talented wordsmiths, pushed me into another direction. Yet, here I am today, pouring my heart into these pages.

Today, I believe that there is someone in this world that needs to read information exactly the way that I write it. I trust that I have a unique blend of qualities to share. I believe that the way that I share my thoughts through my words will have meaning to someone. I hope that someone is you. I believe that my purpose is to share my knowledge and experiences with others. Not everyone will appreciate my style, but my writing is my gift to those who do. I am ok with that. I no longer judge or compare. I trust my purpose and I reject rejection of myself. Even though it took me twenty years to clearly see my passion, I firmly believe that the culmination of all of my life experiences happened perfectly to bring me to where I am doing what I love:

writing, coaching, and speaking. I am now my authentic self.

You can be too. What do you love? What brings you passion and purpose? Are those things part of your life today? If not, how can you incorporate those things into your life? How are you embracing your authentic self? When we embrace our authentic self and live with passion, the fears that have held us back for so long just don't seem all that important anymore. We trust that our inspiration will show us the way. Reject rejection and embrace your authentic self.

Action for Life Exercises

What generalizations do you find yourself making when reacting in fear? How can you re-state these generalizations as facts?

Ask yourself when facing a choice, "Right now, am I acting from a place of fear or a place of love?"

If you were completely confident in your worth, what would you say or do differently? How would your feelings change?

Practice visualizing an event from the past with a perspective of complete trust in your worth. Notice how you feel about yourself, about the situation, and about the other person. How can you see yourself in a new way? What would you say or do differently? How can this process support you in forgiving?

Practice visualizing living under the perspective of your authentic self. Under this perspective, you are living your life doing what you love to do. Say to yourself, "I am unique, special, and unrepeatable. No one else is like me. I bring unique gifts to the world around me." Now notice the details. What are you doing? How do you feel inside? What is your posture? How does your laugh sound? Who do you see? How can you bring this visualization into your reality?

If you feel rejected, what other perspectives can you consider? How are you rejecting yourself? How can you embrace your worth?

Action for Life Team

Who in your life encourages you to be yourself?

Name five people in your life that you can truly be authentic with. What makes them different from everyone else in your life? If you cannot think of five people, what can you do to build authentic relationships?

Who encourages you to follow your passions?

Who encourages you to explore your creative gifts?

Chapter Strategy

Stop taking things personally, making fear-based generalizations, and rejecting yourself. Instead, embrace your humanity, have compassion, and live authentically.

Chapter 5 Key Points

- Embrace unique and discover your authentic self. Embrace all of who you are and the distinctive gifts that are yours alone.

- Our self concept is the way we see ourselves. It is perception based and it changes as we change. It is limited by our perspective at any given moment.

- The Law of Compassion asks us to have compassion for ourselves and others because as we move through the journey of life, we are all just doing the best that we can with the knowledge and skills that we have at any given moment.

- Compassion is turning off the self-critical voice and turning on the self-loving voice. We cannot give compassion to another unless we have it for ourselves. Judgment cannot exist when we have compassion.

- The self-critical voice is the voice of fear.

- Emotional distortions are fear based distortions of facts. They happen when we make broad generalization, use labels, assumptions, and personalizations.

- Rejection can only happen when we reject ourselves. Rejecting ourselves means rejecting our own thoughts, opinions, and needs. It means rejecting what we know to be true about ourselves.

- Rejection simply means that there is not a fit. It does not mean that worth is lessened.

- Forgiveness is a gift to yourself.

- Three important components to feeling forgiveness: acknowledge your feelings, take responsibility for your role, and look for the gifts from the experience.

- Worth is in-born, constant, and can never be diminished.
- We remind ourselves of our worth when we use self-loving language.
- Your authentic self is the real you, the true you. It is the voice of inner wisdom, intuition, and self-love. It is the characteristics, qualities, and gifts that make you uniquely special.
- When you live as your authentic self you feel passion for your life.

Chapter 6

There are No Mistakes, Only Opportunities to Learn

> *"Failure is the greatest opportunity I have to know who I really am."*
> -John Killinger

Fear can be *managed* or *mastered*. Every time we venture outside of our comfort zone and take a risk, we will feel the rush of fear. Unfamiliar territory feels scary to every one of us. Yet, the only way to truly move beyond our fear and build confidence is to face it. When we manage fear, we push it down in an effort to keep it under control, but it often simmers just below the surface causing us to be reactive or defensive. Managing fear is keeping it in check, not facing it. When we manage fear, we are often able to remain functional, but we also remain stuck exactly where we are.

Mastering fear is feeling it and then, taking steps forward anyway. It is deciding to move through the feelings of fear instead of pushing them down in an effort to control them. Mastering fear is deciding to step into the unfamiliar, to be vulnerable, and to choose growth over the perceived safety of our comfort zone. It is choosing action instead of feeling like a hostage to our fear. Mastering fear is deciding that you are in charge of your life.

One of the primary reasons we fail to take risks is because we are afraid to fail. Failing is a blow to the ego. Like fear, it is painful and uncomfortable. Failure *feels* like a personal reflection of who we are. Failure makes us feel inadequate, incompetent, and not good enough; it makes us feel as if we have no control over our destiny. When failure does happen, we often go to great lengths to avoid feeling that way again. We become more cautious, more protective, and more guarded. Yet, in order to truly move forward and create the life that we want, we must be willing to not only risk failing, but to embrace the gifts that failing can bring.

What would you do with your life if fear of failing was not a concern? What would you strive to achieve? How would your behaviors change? Knowing the answers to these questions could change your life in a dramatic way. Fear of failing holds so many of us back from creating the life of our dreams. Even people who have the outward appearance of being successful can harbor fear of failing deep inside.

Richard's Story

Richard was a tall, thirty-something, former athlete who had a great job in sales, a family, and an all around good life. He seemed to be confident, ambitious, and sure of himself. He worked in software sales at a highly reputable company that offered great benefits and great job security. He was a hard working employee who consistently made his sales quota and was always in the top of the sales rankings. To many in the company, he appeared uptight, private, and even aloof at times. These behaviors masked his fears. Staying distant and entertaining only surface conversations was his way of managing his fear. His authentic self was funny, smart, loyal, and outgoing, but he rarely let anyone see that side of him.

After working for this company for about six years, he seemed to become restless. There was a part of him that wanted more: more freedom, more autonomy, and more opportunity. There was another part of him that told him to stay where he was. After all, he made decent money; he had security; and he had good benefits. The more he wrestled with his decision, the more confused he became. Playing into his indecision was that realization that he probably was not going to hit his yearly sales quota and he was intensely afraid to fail. Fear began taking over his thinking and motivating his actions. He worried endlessly about what people would think if he was not successful. What would his managers and colleagues say? Would he be put on probation? Would he lose his job? Would everyone think he was a failure? He wanted to blame everyone else: his manager was a jerk, he got bad accounts, and the product was defective. Placing blame did not relieve his stress or change the reality of his circumstances.

Richard had another job prospect and in fact, received an offer for employment from a riskier, upstart company. This company offered him a 50% increase in salary and much more autonomy. If he took that job, he would have many opportunities to shine, but he would also have the pressure to prove himself. He wondered if he should stay where he was with a secure company enduring the prospect of possible humiliation at year end or should he take the new, riskier job while he had a chance. He could fail there too. No matter where he turned, failure seemed eminent. Fear was in control.

As the time to make a decision grew closer, Richard began to feel more and more stressed and unsure of himself. His voice of fear told him that he was a pretender, a fraud, and a fake. It told him that the success he had achieved in the past was a fluke and that it was just a matter of time before the truth came out. The more he thought about it, the more paralyzed he became. Fear of making the wrong decision dominated his thoughts. He became completely preoccupied with avoiding failure instead of seeking success. He kept weighing the down side of each position and forecasted every possible negative outcome. His fears of rejection and failure intensified. Feelings of anxiety and hopelessness took over his thinking. He literally became paralyzed by his fear and began suffering intense physical symptoms. He could not sleep. He could not eat. He began pacing incessantly. He could not break free from his fear of failing. His fear convinced him that he would fail at either job.

How did someone with a successful sales career and a proven track record get here? For Richard, it had a great deal to with his inability to trust himself. As a former athlete, he was accustomed to getting positive feedback when he performed. Recognition through achievement became the only way for him to feel good about himself. He evaluated himself by the level of positive feedback he received from others. Yet, no matter how much recognition he got, it never seemed to be enough. Even when he did achieve, he was not satisfied because he did not trust his own worth. He was not able to savor the moments of victory. His mind always moved forward to the next challenge, looking for another way to feel good about himself. Winning and achieving became so critically important that he was afraid to lose or fail. In his mind, self-worth and self-trust were tied to his ability to be a top sales performer. The idea of being a non-performer was unthinkable. If he did not perform to expected standards, he would be a failure: deficient and incompetent.

Fear of Failing

Fear of failing is just one of the many factors that keep us doing what we have always done before, but it may be one of the most significant. We get hooked on the idea that we must be sure of a positive outcome before we even try. We fail to take action because we are afraid to fail. We say, "I can't" and then we come up with what we perceive to be a brilliant justification or excuse to uphold our position. Or we try something a few times, justify in our minds that we did try, and then we give up. What if when we were learning to walk as a child, we gave up after trying three times? We would be a society of people crawling around not reaching our potential!

One of the greatest tragedies of the fear of failing is that our thoughts become preoccupied with avoiding failure instead of being open to opportunity. When our thoughts are caught up in avoiding failure, we play it safe and avoid stepping out of our comfort zone. Our fear becomes stronger instead of weaker. We seek to preserve instead of expand. We see failing as the enemy, something we want to avoid at all costs. We represent failure in our minds as a stigma that will haunt us forever and we personalize failure by believing that the failure represents who we are. It is almost as if we secretly imagine that everyone can see "failure" written on our foreheads. Once again, our filters and perceptions play a role in holding us back. Our fear is not our truth. Fear is a perception whose purpose is to keep us safe. Fear is a safety mechanism. There is no real valid foundation for the fear of failing. Fear of failing is simply the fear of the unknown. The reality is none of us can predict exactly what the future holds.

> *Fear of failing is simply the fear of the unknown. The reality is none of us can predict exactly what the future holds.*

The Law of Perfection

If the voice of fear is a coping mechanism, a protector of emotional safety, and it is not the truth, what is the truth? The truth is, inside each of us is a whole, complete, and gifted person--our authentic self. Everything we need to access our greatness and live up to our potential is already within each of us. We all have a special place in the order of life that is ours and ours alone. Within each of our personal journeys is the possibility for passion and excellence. There are no exceptions.

The premise of the Law of Perfection is that we are all experiencing life as a process of evolution. Life is happening *perfectly* in order for us to embrace growth and the fulfillment of our potential. There is only process, growth, and excellence as a result of practice and skill development. When things are not working in our lives, it is a call to action to change our approach. There is no state of "perfection" that we can achieve through our efforts; there is only excellence.

The Law of Perfection is the principle that life is unfolding before us for our greater good. Life is happening to teach us the lessons that we need to learn in order to live the life we are meant to live. Lessons are repeated until we embrace them and make changes. Set backs are a part of the process of learning. They are a part of our progress in learning to trust ourselves. Therefore, we must again be willing to release the "why" from the past and embrace the "how" of the present moment. In our eyes, there may never be a logical reason for why our lives take twists and turns. There may never be logical reason why we experience pain, loss, and sorrow. We must just know in our hearts and minds that the only real answer to "why" is that it creates an opportunity to grow and gain skills that are important for our future. We can ask ourselves, "How can I see this experience as part of my life journey? How can I grow? What can I learn?"

> *Life is happening perfectly in order for us to embrace growth and the fulfillment of our potential. We must ask ourselves:*
> *How can I see this experience as part of my life journey?*
> *What can I learn as a result of this experience?*
> *How can I grow, change, or expand right now?*

Every experience we have happens perfectly for our overall development and growth. Sometimes we do not see what life is teaching us. When we are resistant to learning, the lessons become more challenging. What you resist persists. Life speaks in whispers at first. If you do not hear, it knocks a little louder. If you still do not listen, Life yells at you, loud and clear. I believe that in my case, when I was on bed rest waiting for my daughter to arrive, the lesson was to slow down and take care of myself. I was miserable because I could not get up and "do". Instead of being peaceful and enjoying the rest, I bemoaned every moment. After she was born, I got back to my routine of doing, proving, and giving to feel worthy. I did not hear my life lesson until I had ended up sick in bed with exhaustion a few years later. I heard when Life yelled. Today, I truly understand that everything happens for a reason.

The Law of Perfection reminds us that success and failure are subjective terms that we individually assign meaning to. They do not define who we are, but merely whether or not we have reached our desired objectives. One cannot be a success or a failure as a person. A "success" or a "failure" implies that personal worth has changed and we already know that worth is constant. In reality, there are only causes and effects and there are actions that bring about results. All effects or results can be traced back to a cause and all causes lead to effects. Life is a journey that teaches us to learn how to create the results that we seek.

Redefine Failing

Life is complex and things don't always go the way we want or expect them to. Road blocks, challenges, and obstacles are a part of life. They are going to happen. No one goes through life without facing problems or experiencing some level of misfortune. People may face different degrees of challenge, but no one is immune. It is how we handle obstacles and challenges that determine our future. As with every aspect of our lives, we have a choice. We can buckle under pressure. We can resist the reality of the situation and see adversity as a roadblock. We can keep repeating the same behavior over and over and getting the same result. We can choose to remain angry and place blame on everyone or everything outside of ourselves. We can internalize our feelings and endlessly beat ourselves up or just outright quit trying. Or we can see failure in a new light. We can see failure as a gift that teaches us lessons that are critical to our overall growth.

Basketball superstar, Michael Jordon once said, "I've missed more than 9000 shots in my career. I've lost almost 300 games. 26 times, I've been trusted to take the winning shot and missed. I've failed over and over and over again in my life. And that's why I succeed." Every experience we have teaches us something about ourselves. Learning cannot move backwards; we cannot unlearn knowledge. Once we have it, it is ours to keep. We can choose to embrace any experience as an investment in ourselves. We can choose to face adversity head on or we can resist it by pondering "why" life is unfair.

> *One of the greatest tragedies of the fear of failing is that our thoughts become preoccupied with avoiding failure instead of being open to opportunity. Our fear is not our truth.*

Failure and adversity can be our greatest teachers. We must be willing to see the discomfort as a temporary experience and believe that "this too shall pass". The past is gone and all we have is the present. We must be willing to see that the adversity will be a gift and we will gain from having persevered. The feelings that go along with adversity and failure are temporary, but the knowledge and wisdom we gain from the experience will last forever. Instead of fearing adversity, we can embrace it as an opportunity to improve our knowledge base and enhance our skill sets. Failure can actually augment our learning process if we are willing to be open to the gifts of adversity.

There are ten major gifts that adversity creates. The first is that it creates opportunities to learn and improve. For example, an employee that has used an ineffective approach in the past can learn more effective ways to convey his ideas. He can gain wisdom and he can build his skills. He can keep trying until he finds a method that is effective. Facing adversity also enhances our ability to become resilient. We cannot develop resiliency without facing challenges. When we rise to the challenge, we learn that we can handle whatever comes our way and we build self-trust. We gain the ability to fall and get back up again. We learn that there is no shame in failing because failing is a temporary set back.

Adversity challenges us to think out of the box and get creative. It challenges us to use the power of our thoughts to seek new solutions and innovations. Some of the greatest scientific breakthroughs in history came about as a result of adversity. Even in personal relationships, facing adversity together can bring about a deep sense of connection that would not have otherwise happened. When we face adversity, we step outside of our comfort zone. When we step outside of our comfort zone and risk, we build self-confidence. As we build self-confidence, we gain the ability to rely on ourselves to work through challenges instead of running away from them or giving up.

Adversity creates the ability to see new possibilities in the road ahead. It opens the door to seeing alternate paths. Sometimes when we set a goal, we think we have a very clear vision of what each step forward will look like. Yet, when adversity pops up, we may find that there are alternate paths to get to where we want to go that we had not seen before. For example, Susan was negotiating her employment agreement. She strongly desired a specific base salary. The employer came back to her and told her that they could not meet her salary requirements. Susan and her potential employer were at a stand still. Susan came to me for coaching support. She asked me to help her get what she wanted. Together, Susan and I mapped out her true priorities and Susan decided to consider an alternate path. She was willing to accept the lower base salary, if they were willing to give her a small car allowance, an extra week of vacation, and flex time. In the end, both parties were thrilled with the results.

Adversity can also provide motivation to push beyond any perceived personal limitations. We think that we would not be able to handle a challenge until we are actually faced with it. Then, we find out how strong we really are. When challenges come up, we learn more about how to be responsible for our lives and our happiness. For instance, no one wants to be put in the position of fighting cancer, but faced with that challenge, we see extraordinary examples of strength and courage. Pain and adversity can take us to places we would never choose to go on our own, but also give us wisdom and perspective that we would not have gained either. There are many people who choose to live with more purpose and intention because of such an experience and they go on to positively impact the lives of others by sharing their insights.

We also learn that while failure or an undesired outcome may have been the end result, there were gifts along the journey. There were things that did work, that did go right, or that taught us something. There were successes, or the attainment of some goals, along the way. Our knowledge and wisdom grew. Therefore, the reward truly lies in the process of taking action and moving forward. The action is the true teacher, not the actual outcome.

Gifts adversity creates:

Opportunities to learn and improve

Resilience and self-trust to handle challenges

Out of the box thinking, mind power, and innovation

Self-confidence as a result of stepping out of comfort zone

Self-reliance

Ability to see the possibilities of a new path

Motivation to push beyond perceived limits

Enhanced personal responsibility

Focus on successes within each journey

Focus on the process, instead of outcomes

See Failing with New Eyes

As long as we are open, there are great gifts to be learned in every experience, whether or not we define the experience as a success or a failure. With every experience, we get to make an investment in ourselves. When we invest in ourselves, we are really learning to maximize our capabilities. We get to expand our skills, to learn, to grow, and to uncover strengths that we did not know we had. We get to see new perspectives, gain new insights, and learn more about ourselves. With each project, relationship, or new adventure, we take the investment we make in ourself with us. It is ours to keep. No matter what the experience is, our skills, knowledge, and confidence stay with us.

Since there is a gift in every experience, we can choose to classify *every* experience as beneficial. Every experience is teaching us something that we needed to learn. Instead of using the words success and failure, we can choose to use the words "cause and effect" or "action and result". If we define success and failure along the lines of action and result, we no longer personalize those words. Failure is an undesired result and success is a desired result. We no longer personalize because we separate the person and the event. The person is not and can never be "a failure". If the results were undesired, then we can change the actions that brought about those results. We can consider alternate paths to follow to get a different result. Sometimes we learn more from our missteps than from our successes. It is all part of the process of learning.

We can also choose to redefine the words success and failure based upon the process, not the outcome. For example, we could choose to attach meaning like this: as long as we move forward in our process, we are successful. As long as we gain

> *A "success" or a "failure" implies that personal worth has changed and we already know that worth is constant.*

knowledge or skills, we have achieved our goal. What if success means doing the absolute best that you can do, nothing more and nothing less? How would your life change if you redefined these words? Failure could mean: failing to try or giving up, instead of falling short of a goal. For me, failure means giving up and I know I will never give up. Therefore, I can never fail.

When we release our fixation on the words success and failure, the process of achieving our desires becomes a journey of exploration and curiosity. We no longer focus on avoiding failure, but seeking excellence. We become excited to see how the journey will unfold without attaching to a specific result. We become open to unexpected possibilities presenting themselves. We see the journey as trial and error, gaining knowledge about what moves us closer to our desired outcome. Focusing on the process of moving forward with intention and commitment, frees us from our fear of failing. Undesired results simply give us feedback and inspire us to change course instead of succumbing to our fear. We can take action; evaluate the progress; adjust our course; and take new action.

Win-Win Decision Making

One of the hallmarks of fear of failing is the inability to make a decision. Many of us make a strong association in our minds that the right decision will bring us happiness and peace of mind and the wrong decision will create failure and loss. We get stuck in over analysis paralysis, where we weigh the pros and cons of each decision such that we become completely paralyzed by the decision making process. Again, all of our perceptions stem from our thoughts. If our thoughts are based in fear, fear of making the wrong decision, we will continue to second guess any decision we make. When we decide to see everything happening perfectly in order to enhance our learning process, fear is no longer in control. As we see adversity in a new way, we must be willing to see decision making in a new way.

Now that we are clear that there are benefits in every experience we have, we can use the Win-Win decision model. In this model, there is no such thing as a wrong decision. Each choice has benefits. Each choice provides unique opportunities. Within each choice are important lessons to be learned and gifts to be gained. This model enables us to create a new perspective of our decision making process and trust that every experience will teach us something new.

When we are faced with making a decision, we must first do our homework. We want to go into the decision making process armed with as much information as we can gather. Next, we list the perceived positives, benefits, and gifts that you will receive along the way for each of the possible choices. Decide what aspect or aspects of the decision have the most meaning or value to you. For example, you may decide that a job that offers travel is more important to you than a job that offers flex time. Rate the top three benefits that have the most value. See each decision as a path or journey in which you will receive gifts of knowledge and experience. Both paths offer benefits and because of those benefits, either path is a winning choice. Any path you choose will offer you gifts and you cannot make a wrong decision.

Win-Win Model

Choice A:

Benefits + Knowledge + Experience = Win

Choice B:

Benefits + Knowledge + Experience = Win

Because life happens perfectly for our greatest development, either path will offer benefits and insights. Not every action will lead you to a specific desired outcome, but you will gain more knowledge about how to get there.

Changing Course

It is impossible to create excellence without effort. It is impossible to make true effort without risk. It is impossible to take risk without jumping out of your comfort zone. How do we find the courage to break free of our self-limiting beliefs and embrace risk on a daily basis? We have learned many tools so far. We can release disempowering expectations and focus on what is within our scope of influence. We can embrace personal responsibility for creating our best life. We can take action based on our commitments and intentions. We can make a choice based on the Win-Win Model. We can trust ourselves to handle anything that comes our way in life.

I said earlier that the fear of failing often moves us into preservation mode instead of expansion mode. The true battle lies within our minds. When we do not have self-trust, we fear that making the wrong move or the wrong decision is going to cause our lives to collapse. Again, fear based thinking is not reality based thinking. The reality is that we each have an innate ability to handle anything that comes our way, if we focus on trusting ourselves and receiving the gifts in every experience. Our ability is inborn and ever present. As long as we are alive, we can continue to grow and part of growing is practicing trusting ourselves. We do grow stronger with every experience.

I am a huge believer in focusing on the positives in any given situation, but sometimes my clients need to talk through their worst case scenario in order to begin to trust themselves. The goal here is to help the client see that they can handle any result or outcome. In the case of my client Blake, he was terrified of losing his job. He had severe blood pressure problems and his doctors suggested that he take some time off or even consider short term disability. In our coaching sessions, he kept telling me that he cannot take time off because he could not risk losing his job. Here is a part of our dialogue:

OK, so what if you lose your job? Then what?

Then, I won't be able to pay my bills.

OK, you won't be able to pay your bills. Then what?

Then, I risk losing my house.

OK, you risk losing your house. Then what?

Then, I might have to sell my house.

OK, you sell your house. Then what?

I could lose money.

OK, you lose money. Then what?

I would be a "nobody" lying in the gutter.

Is that really true or are you making it up? Would you really be a "nobody" with no place to go? Would you really lie in the gutter?

No, but everything I worked for would be gone. I would not be able to afford another house and I'd have to rent.

Everything would be gone? How would your knowledge and skills be gone?

They would not, but I still would not have any money.

What can you do with knowledge and skills?

Make money.

You get the idea. As we continued to work through the worst case scenario, Blake realized that his fear had no real basis. He realized that he could deal with any scenario that happened in his life. There was absolutely nothing that he could not handle or bounce back from. Once we began to establish his self-trust, we began to rebuild the same scenario and focus on possibilities and opportunities.

You have lost your job, sold your home, and are renting somewhere. Now what?

I guess I get to look for a new job.

What would that look like?

I can find a job that I really love: a job where I can be more creative and autonomous.

What are the benefits of finding a job with more creativity and autonomy?

I would be really happy.

What does happiness bring you?

Peace of mind, fulfillment.

What are the benefits of the current financial situation?

Paying the bills and the mortgage is no longer pressuring me the way it was before.

How does this impact your job search?

It offers me freedom to choose to do what I really want to do.

How does the worst case scenario look from this perspective?

It looks like an option that offers me opportunity, instead of loss.

I do not want to over simplify. Clearly Blake was facing some significant changes. However, his focus on fear based thinking was not empowering him to take charge of the situation. Again, once we move away from fear based thinking, we open ourselves to possibility. The fear does not master us; we master the fear and we see that we can handle any challenge that comes our way. Our thoughts create our reality.

Always Do Your Best

Life is a journey. Like a river that has twists and turns, so do our lives. The water flowing in the river moves around the rocks and obstacles. There are days when the current is faster and there are days when the current is slower. No matter what, it never ceases to flow and move forward. So, the river can be a great model for our lives. Obstacles and challenges are inevitable for each of us, but we can choose to trust ourselves to move through, over, and around our challenges. People who are able to achieve their dreams actually fail more often than other people. Why? Because they take more risks, fall down, and pick them selves back up again and again. They are willing to take steps forward even in the face of obstacles and adversity. They focus on solutions rather than on problems. They see every challenge as an opportunity to do their best and to gain more insight. We can all choose to keep moving forward toward our desired result. Along the way, all we can ever really do is offer our best effort. Our best effort is the most that we can ever give at any moment.

When we do our best, we feel good about ourselves. We are not focused on any specific outcome and we are not tied up in disempowering expectations. We take action because we want to, not because we have to. We are choosing to act through our commitment to give the best of ourselves. We do our best because we are doing what we love to do. We do our best because it feels right, not because we have expectations of receiving something in return. Focusing on doing our best lifts our self-trust and our self-esteem. When we focus on doing our best, we turn off the negative self-talk in our head. We turn off the voice of self-judgment. The voice cannot criticize or condemn us for giving the best effort that we can give at any time. There is no beating ourselves up and there are no regrets.

As I said in chapter two, life expands through risk and action. A dream is just a dream, unless we are willing to take action. Fear of failing melts away when we decide to live our lives by simply doing our best. Really living is about taking action: Action for Life. Inaction perpetuates our fear and withholds us from a rewarding life. Dreams start in the mind. We can have the most amazing ideas, but without action, our ideas remain ideas. A dream is simply a dream, unless you are willing to take action and give it your best shot. We cannot let fear of failing stop us from taking steps to turn our dreams into reality. Defining our choices by doing our best gives us the freedom to risk and take chances without fearing failure. We can strive for excellence and release the desire for the perfect outcome.

Trust in Self

You remember Richard from the beginning of this chapter. Richard decided to take some time off of work to decide what he really wanted to do with his life and what his priorities were. He wanted to figure out what was behind the fear, address it, and begin creating the career that he knew he was meant to have. Richards's desire to achieve his goals was an admirable quality, but he knew that the fear of failing that left him paralyzed would never get him to where he wanted to go. Richard knew that it was time to look at fear, failure, and success in a new way.

Richard wanted to change his fear-based thinking, but he felt he needed to really figure out who he was and what he wanted. He stayed in his current position for a few more months and paid attention to all of the things he did well and all of the strengths he had. He made a conscious effort to listen to his inner wisdom instead of relying on validation from others. Richard even decided to share his encounter with fear with his co-workers. He wanted to take his social masks off once and for all and just be a real person who faced his fear.

He was amazed by the genuine support and connection he felt with others by being himself. People did not judge his imperfections; they embraced his courage to be true to himself. Richard challenged his fear by rejecting old beliefs that he knew were not true. Whenever doubt crept into his mind, he questioned his thinking and asked, "What is my truth?" He began to see very clearly that all of the skills, talents, and gifts he needed to be successful were within him. He knew that it was his thoughts, not his skills and talents, which were holding him back. A key realization for Richard was that he was not taking full and complete responsibility for creating his life. He was not living authentically.

Richard had always wanted to run his own business. He made a plan, took steps forward one day at a time, and less than a year later intentionally left his job. Today, he is a successful business consultant with a thriving business. He learned to trust himself, take risks without expectations, and focus on his passion. Now, he anticipates challenges with enthusiasm. He has re-defined what success and failure mean to him. He knows that there are gifts in every experience. He knows that the benefits of adversity are countless and he uses results as a guide in charting his course. He no longer defines his actions in terms of success and failure; he sees them in terms of cause and effect. In his mind, he is a success because he has found his passion and wakes up excited for the new day ahead.

> The feelings that go along with adversity and failure are temporary, but the knowledge and wisdom we gain from the experience will last forever.

Keys to Trusting Yourself

Fear based thinking is always a call to action because we cannot be our authentic self and live our best life while consumed by fear. There are several key signs to look for when you are learning to trust yourself. When we trust ourselves, we gain a willingness to take risks without fearing failure. Failure is simply an undesired result, but it is not a reflection of who we are as a human being. Failure does not reflect a person; it reflects an outcome or event. Fear of failing is a call to action to choose another course or to take a different path. It is not an invitation to give up.

You have heard the saying that "Winners never quit and quitters never win," by Vince Lombardi. We develop self-trust when we allow ourselves to risk falling and we learn how to pick ourselves back up again. Whether or not we finish the race first does not matter. It is the act of finishing, learning, and following through that builds our self-esteem. We build self-trust when we follow through and complete what we started, even if the result is not the result that we were hoping for. A sense of completion builds self-trust. We can give ourselves credit for the successes along the way instead of focusing on the end result. Doing our best is all we can ever do.

We develop trust in ourselves when we realize that there is nothing that we cannot handle. Whatever adversity or challenges lie ahead, we will make a plan and do our best to achieve a desired result. No matter what, we will learn from the experience and we will gain knowledge. There is no experience that we cannot gain from. We can take full and complete responsibility for creating our life, our happiness, and our future. We do not blame, make excuses, or wear social masks. We no longer need to hide behind those things because we are willing to create an authentic life. When we face adversity instead of being fearful, we welcome the opportunity to grow. We have compassion for what we have not yet learned and for our imperfections.

We can choose to embrace even the most challenging circumstances or people and see the challenges as gifts. We can be grateful for what we get to learn. We can be grateful for the opportunity to develop new skills. When we are willing to see the gifts in every experience, we are saying yes to life and all that it brings. We can choose to see every event and every experience, whether good or bad, as a life lesson designed to teach us more about ourselves.

Action for Life Exercises

What would you attempt if fear of failing was not an issue?

What would living fully look like?

What would you gain by taking steps toward your desired result?

Who could you meet?

What could you learn?

How would your skills grow?

What decisions have you been wrestling with?

What obstacles are you facing?

How could you re-state the challenges as goals?

How can you see each of your choices in the Win-Win Model?

One year from now, what do you want to have accomplished to feel like you have done your best?

What are potential obstacles?

What are potential opportunities?

What skills or strengths do you already have and what skills do you need to build?

How will you do that?

What are the benefits of taking action?

What are the costs of not taking action?

Action for Life Team

Who can you rely on for support when facing adversity?

Who has already faced a similar challenge that would be a resource to you?

Who can you add to your team to make it more complete?

Chapter Strategy

Turn adversity and fear of failing into opportunities to grow. See life as happening perfectly to help you strive for excellence.

Chapter 6 Key Points

- There are no mistakes, only opportunities to learn.

- The Law of Perfection states that life is happening perfectly to teach us the skills that we need to learn in order to fulfill our potential.

- Life is a process based journey filled with experiences. There are gifts in every experience.

- One of the greatest tragedies of the fear of failing is that our thoughts become preoccupied with avoiding failure instead of being open to opportunity.

- There is no state of "perfection" that we can achieve through our efforts; there is only excellence.

- Learning cannot move backwards; we cannot unlearn knowledge.

- Facing adversity creates many benefits: opportunities to improve, innovation, building self-confidence and self-reliance, motivation, and personal responsibility.

- Failure cannot exist as long as we view an experience as a teacher.

- Redefine success and failure. There are only actions and results.

- The most we can ever give at any moment is our best effort.

- When we develop self-trust, we realize that we can handle anything that comes our way.

Chapter 7

Attitude is Everything. Live In Gratitude.

"When we choose to focus not on what is missing from our lives but are grateful for the abundance that's present... we experience heaven on earth."—Sarah Ban Breathnach

"My friend Jane said coaching helped her, but I don't have any fear. I am not really sure why I called you. I am very responsible for my life and I run my own business. I have many friends. I have a great attitude, but I am also realistic. I have given up on meeting Mr. Right, but I am ok with that. I don't complain or make excuses; I just accept that this is how my life was meant to be," said Kayla. "When I go out, I go out with friends and I don't feel the need to meet other people. Making small talk is so boring and I would rather not even bother. What a waste of time! I am content with my life just the way it is. Men are intimidated by independent women like me and when it comes right down to it they only want one thing anyway. I know from past experience. The only guys out there that are still single are the ones that no one else wants. It is slim pickings out there. They all have some kind of weird hang up like only dating blondes or drinking to excess. Trust me, I am good with my life just the way it is."

Kayla sure said a great deal about her beliefs in a short amount of time. If Kayla had not made complaints, judgments, and justifications, I might have believed that she was content being single, but her words advertised that fear was dominating her thinking. Kayla had been burned in the past and was not interested in being vulnerable. She was not approachable and she was not willing to approach anyone else. She was not willing to look at how her own behaviors created her reality and she focused on what is wrong instead of what is right. Her attitude reflected her beliefs.

Our attitude is the way in which we view our lives. It is our overall frame of mind, disposition, and outlook. Our attitude is a significant component of our belief system and it influences the way we approach the world. It affects every relationship we have, both personally and professionally. It affects our desire to risk and break out of our comfort zone. It affects our determination, our efforts, and our ability to persevere. It sounds cliché, but there are two primary attitudes or ways we look at the world: optimistic or pessimistic. An optimistic perspective is aligned with love, peacefulness, and being our authentic self. A pessimistic perspective is aligned with fear and our fearful self. Our thoughts and actions generally fall into one of these two categories.

Love and fear are the two primary energies that motivate our thoughts, feelings, and actions. Love and fear are mutually exclusive. We either see the world from a benevolent perspective, where the world is filled with love and trust or a malevolent perspective, where we see the world as hostile and out to get us. We see the glass as half full or we see the glass half empty. We feel that we have the ability to create our lives or we feel as if we have no control and we are victims of whatever comes our way. Whatever we believe, we build evidence to support our beliefs in order to justify in our minds that our beliefs are valid. What do you believe? Do you believe that the world is for you or against you? How sure are you of your answer?

An optimistic viewpoint is a generally benevolent view of life and the world. There is a fundamental belief that the world is "for" us and that life is happening in a way that will propel us forward. Life is not filled with struggle, but opportunities to learn. Abundance is everywhere. A benevolent view is in alignment with hope and possibility. A person with an optimistic outlook is open to whatever lies on the road ahead. They have a willingness to explore and be curious about the gifts in every experience.

A pessimistic viewpoint or way of looking at the world is more a malevolent view. These people feel as if life is against us and struggle is the norm. People with a malevolent view are consumed by all of the suffering, misfortune, and injustice in the world. They tend to go through life feeling that there is no fairness, no equity in the world. They have strong self imposed limitations about what is possible for them. Their self-limiting beliefs keep them from breaking out and taking the action that will change their lives. They often see no value in even trying to do anything differently because they have already decided that there is no point, no possibility of anything working out the way they want it to.

I want to make an important distinction. People can have an optimistic attitude in one area of their life and be pessimistic in another area. For example, Kayla felt confidence and mastery in her professional life, but displayed fear and pessimism in her love life. Make sure to pay attention to what areas of your life are really working and what areas are not. Examine the thoughts and feelings that are present in each area. Notice the differences in how you approach areas of your life where you feel more confident versus areas where you do not.

I have found that when I ask people if they think that they

are optimistic or pessimistic, very few people will admit to having a pessimistic outlook. Socially, there is a negative connotation attached to being pessimistic. People usually try to tell me that although they might not be optimistic, they classify themselves as a "realist", someone who is realistic about the struggles of life. Life is not always easy. I fully acknowledge that. Yet, if it weren't for fear, we could not know courage. If it weren't for challenge, we could not know resilience. I am all for accepting the reality of life, but there really is a difference in how we respond to that reality with our thoughts and actions that reflects our true inner attitudes. Operating from a fear based perspective is not in alignment with our authentic self.

Our inner attitudes are expressed outwardly in a variety of ways that we may not be fully aware of. I have said that fear can be very subtle and insidious. Negative attitudes can be the same way. You may think you are a positive person, but hidden expectations of negative experiences are holding you back. Let's consider an example. Imagine that you have been invited to attend a conference in two weeks and in the spur of the moment, you accept the invitation and pay the registration fee. On the day of the conference, what are you thinking and feeling?

> 1) As you arrive at the registration desk, there is a small crowd chatting and laughing. You are patient at first, but then become annoyed because they are being so inconsiderate. They are taking too long and totally ignoring you. You finally give your name, sign in, and take a seat in the back of the room. You wonder what possessed you to sign up for this conference in the first place. You knew it was a mistake. You look around the room observing others and forming opinions about them. You say to yourself, "Boy, that guy must need attention, look at how loud he is talking. Look at how that woman is

dressed; does she think this is a beach party? Hmm. There is nothing to eat. I wish I had known. I would have eaten before I left." As you look around, you really start to feel like you do not fit in because no one is talking to you. A couple sits down next to you and instead of acknowledging your presence, they continue talking as if you don't even exist. They can clearly see that you are alone and you wonder why they cannot at least say hello. You pretend to read the brochure you received so that you will look like you are doing something important. As people walk down your row to fill in the last seats, you lean back to get out of the way while keeping your head down. You feel very alone and you think the people here are rude. You knew you should not have signed up for this conference. You knew this was going to be a waste of time and you feel so disappointed by the type of people you have encountered.

2) As you arrive at the registration desk, a small crowd is chatting and laughing. You think that the conference looks like it is going to be a lot of fun. You wait patiently and as you are waiting, you decide to join in on the fun and interject a comment. You share a laugh with the people at the table. You give your name, sign in, and choose a seat where you will be able to see everything. You are excited for the possibilities. You scan the room to look for people you think you would like to meet. You hear a man talking loudly and you think he has great energy and presence. You have not met anyone yet, but you are looking forward it. You called ahead and found out food was not going to be served, so you had a snack before you came. A couple sits down next to you and they are deep in conversation. You realize that they are not ignoring you; they are just listening intently to each other. You decide to make conversation with

the person in the next row by asking a question. He politely answers your question and then turns back around. You decide to introduce yourself to someone else. After talking with her, you learn that you actually have several things in common. As people filter down your row, you look up and smile. You knew attending this conference was a stretch for you personally, but you feel proud of yourself for stepping out of your box and attending on your own. You knew this experience was going to bring you so many gifts.

Which scenario is most reflective of your thoughts and actions? Do you create a positive experience with your attitude or do you perceive that the world is against you and build evidence to prove it? Do you focus on taking advantage of opportunities in the moment and actively participate or do you focus on what you think other people should be doing? Which scenario reflects a "realist" perspective? Both situations are entirely realistic. Yet, the attitude of approach was very different for each scenario. Attitude matters. Attitude is a component of our belief system and our beliefs are profoundly powerful. We create a self-fulfilling prophecy with our attitudes and beliefs. We use everything we see, feel, and experience to validate our position. The person in scenario 1 went in expecting the experience to be a waste of time and they unconsciously took action to support that attitude. The person in scenario 2 experienced identical circumstances to the person in scenario 1, but their attitude created a positive overall experience. In other words, your attitude creates your reality and reflects your willingness to participate in any situation as it is, instead of bemoaning what it is not.

Our overall way of looking at life and the thoughts we focus on, create our actions and our reality. Our thoughts are at the core of everything we see, feel, and do. As I have said so many times, our thoughts create our reality. So, when we choose our attitude toward any situation, we choose what we will experience. Attitudes are an outward expression of our internal thoughts. Are you willing to embrace the world as it is or do you choose to begrudge it for what it is not? The choice is within you. When you have a negative attitude, the question becomes is the world against you or are *YOU* against you? The answer is *you* are against you. You are creating your reality. You can meet people; you can enjoy yourself; and you can interact with an approachable posture. You can stop judging and release expectations. You can see life as happening perfectly in order to help you build skills and gain knowledge. You can stop complaining and find gratitude for what is.

Everything is Wrong

It seems that so many people focus on everything that is wrong in the world instead of everything that is right. We are impatient. We hold onto grievances. We focus on our aches, pains, and suffering. We see life as an endless struggle. We step into seeing the world as against us and say things like, "I am so unlucky. Things just don't work out for me. Life is so hard." We justify our position and build proof that our perceptions are right. We act as if our misery bonds us together. We talk about how awful and unfair life is. Joe complains about his bad back, the commute to work, and the weather. Amanda complains about her boyfriend and the inequities in their relationship. Alex complains about the cost of gasoline, the government, and how his boss expects him to work late. We agree with each other and nod in sympathy. We focus so much energy on what is wrong. The evening news reports tragedy after tragedy. We talk about it the next day by the water cooler. After we leave the water cooler, we tell our friends and repeat the same stories over and over again. You know people like this—maybe you are one. It is no wonder so many people are down in the dumps!

Complaining is taking life for granted. It is an attitude of lack and scarcity. It is focusing on what is wrong instead of what is right. Complaining targets problems, not solutions and prevents us from taking constructive action. Yes, there are challenges in life, but what good does it do us to focus so much time and energy on what is wrong if we are not going to do anything about it? Complaining helps fear stay in control. When we complain, we repeat the problem over and over again. We live in it. We wallow in it. We build evidence that we are right and convince others to agree with us so that we can feel even more righteous. When we complain, we focus all of our energy on what we perceive the problem to be. Since our thoughts ultimately create our reality, we continue to create more problems by complaining.

Complaining strengthens fear by keeping us feeling powerless, as if we have no control over our lives. Complaining is failing to be responsible for what we experience in our lives. It is a form of denial and escapism. Let's face it. Complaining is the easy way out. When we get stuck in our complaints, we are actually announcing to the world that we are not feeling good about ourselves and our ability to be in charge of our life. Yet, we are paying a huge price, when we choose irresponsibility, escapism, and negative thought patterns.

When we focus only on what is wrong, we also tend to move into other disempowering behaviors, such as judging, blaming, and jealousy. These are the "should" actions where we have a specific view of how we think things should be. We are making up a personal rule book and expecting everyone else to live by our rules. When we say comments like, "My management team is completely inept; if my spouse was not so lazy, our marriage would be better; or my friend acts like she is better than me because she drives a sports car.", we are phrasing our statements as complaints, but what we are really saying is that we think people should be different than they are. Instead of looking at the way we interact, we are judging how we think others should be.

Discontent comes from within, even when you think it is about someone or something else. Instead of complaining about what is wrong, be willing to look at yourself, accept the reality of what is, look for solutions, or appreciate what is right. I am not suggesting that we become passive or complacent. I am suggesting that you look around and see what is possible and what is good in this very moment. What are you learning from this moment? What actions are you committed to taking right here, right now? The weight of discontent and dissatisfaction evaporate when we see the gifts in *what is* and we choose to live in the present moment. When we choose our thoughts, our emotions follow. We cannot change negative feelings by focusing on what is wrong, missing, or bad. We cannot access our authentic self when we choose thoughts that are in alignment with fear and scarcity. What if we really paid attention to the good in every experience? How would our belief systems begin to shift?

The Law of Gratitude

What if every time we had a complaint or a judgment, we instead found gratitude and we looked for the gifts in the experience? We cannot find inner peace when we focus on what is wrong and we cannot access our authentic self when we are in fear. Gratitude helps us clearly see what is right. Gratitude shifts us into a calmer place and helps us focus on what is working instead of what is not working. When we are willing to be open, we see a life filled with abundance, not lack. We see the world as for us, not against us. An attitude of gratitude enables us to have compassion for ourselves and others. It creates a sense of understanding and peacefulness for the reality of the moment. It enables us to release our expectations of what we think "should be" and accept what is.

Lack of gratitude actually blocks good things from coming to us. As soon as we become grateful for what we already have, we begin to attract more abundance to our lives. We attract more to be grateful for. The more grateful we are, the more we see things to be grateful for. We can focus on gratitude for all things, big and small. I am grateful that I have the ability to make choices every day. I am grateful traffic reminds me to slow down and live in the present moment. I am grateful that I am able to feel a loving touch from my husband. Every time we have a complaint or a judgment, we can choose to shift our thinking into gratitude. Having gratitude may be the single most powerful exercise in shifting our attitudes.

> *When we choose our thoughts, our emotions follow. Complaining strengthens fear by keeping us feeling powerless, as if we have no control over our lives. Complaining targets problems, not solutions and prevents us from taking constructive action. Having gratitude may be the single most powerful exercise in shifting our attitudes.*

Enlightened by Gratitude

A few summers ago, we were heading to our annual family trip to the beach. We go every year with my husband's entire family. My children look forward this vacation with great anticipation each and every time. This particular year, my husband was tying up some loose ends at work, so I decided to pack the luggage and load the family van myself. It was a sweltering hot, August day. We bring just about everything, but the kitchen sink to the beach: beach shoes, swim shoes, sheets and towels, books and toys, boogie boards, beach umbrellas, beach chairs, clothing for days, clothing for evenings, food and beverages, and on and on. After some creative positioning of the luggage, we were all ready to hit the road for our five hour trip. I was in the passenger seat, all strapped in and ready to go. I turned around to face the back seat and ask my children a question.

All of a sudden, I felt this wave of pain shoot up my back. I felt each muscle in my back ripple and tighten. I was in intense pain. I had thrown my back out and I could not move. As I gasped at the pain, my family froze with anxiety and bewilderment. Four pairs of eyes, as large as saucers, were staring at me, waiting for me to say something. Just breathing was painful and I was not sure what to do. Since we were already in the car, I asked my husband to drive to one of those emergency clinics. When we arrived in the parking lot, it seemed like it took me thirty minutes just to get out of the van. I shuffled slowly into the doctor's office, signed in, and stood in the corner leaning on a chair.

To this day, I could not tell you what my doctor's face looked like. I was hunched over, unable to stand upright, and all I could see was his shoes. I could tell you all about his shoes because I stood there so long looking at them. They were brown and shiny and I could almost see my reflection in them. I laughed to myself, "Nice shoes for a Saturday morning." Laughter eased my pain. The doctor prescribed medication and ice. My husband ran into the nearest pharmacy and then we started making our way to the beach.

As we drove, I berated myself for being so stupid. "Why did I do this to myself?" my negative voice shouted. I found myself thinking about all of the things I could not do on our trip. I wondered why I had been so careless and lifted heavy luggage. I beat myself up for not taking better care of myself when I knew better. I made small talk with my family, but my thoughts kept drifting back to how my vacation was ruined. I thought about all of the things I could not do and all of the experiences I would miss. I thought about how I would be stuck laying down, unable to move. I felt guilty because I believed I had let my kids down. When we got to the beach, I cried a big cry, partly from pain and partly from frustration. I settled in on the couch and watched everyone else laugh and talk, play in the pool, and explore the house. I was feeling pretty darn sorry for myself.

Later that evening, I had a talk with myself and chose to look for gratitude in the situation. Boy, it was hard at first! I am not kidding. The pain was intense and it was very easy to be miserable. I decided to write my feelings of gratitude in my journal. As I sat there looking at a blank page, the only thing I could think of being grateful for at the time was a soft couch to sit on. "It is better than being in a tent", I told myself. Clearly, this was going to be quite a challenge, but I was up for it. I wanted to think different thoughts. I wanted to feel differently about the situation. I committed to writing ten things each day specifically about my current situation that I was grateful for.

I noted that my dinner had been brought to me. That was something to be grateful for. Other people cooked and did the dishes. That was cool. It was pretty quiet where I was sitting. That was a treat for me. The more I sat in the stillness of the moment and cleared my mind of the negative clutter, the more I could see the gifts all around me. The flood gates of gratitude opened up and poured out of me. I am grateful I have the opportunity to stay at the beach with my husband's family. I am grateful I can hear the sound my children's laughter and the excitement in their squeals of joy. I am grateful that I get to rest and read a great book. I am grateful that I get to take long naps. I had not done that since before my kids came along. I am grateful that I am being waited on and taken care of. I am grateful that I have full clicker control and can watch my favorite show uninterrupted. I am grateful that my kids are learning to be more independent and finding their own stuff. I am grateful that I can hear the relaxing sound of the ocean from my room. I am grateful; I am grateful; I am grateful…I wrote over sixty different things that I was grateful for.

Once I shifted my thinking, my grey gloom turned to bright, vivid, happy colors. My circumstances did not change. I was on that couch for six full days. What changed was my thinking. When I changed my thinking from complaints to gratitude, I found inner peace and genuine happiness. To this day, I will remember that vacation as one of my best ever. I enjoyed being in the moment, exactly where I was with what I had. It was a light bulb event that changed me forever. I experienced first hand how powerful gratitude really is. I had always seen myself as someone who was grateful and who appreciated the blessings I had in my life. I found that real gratitude goes even deeper than that. The kind of gratitude I am talking about now is gratitude from my soul. This kind of gratitude has no limits. It is detailed and abundant and joyous. Once I felt its power, it became clear that my thoughts truly create the quality of my life.

Release Emotions through Venting

Feelings are a reflection of our thoughts, but there are no bad or wrong feelings. When we feel hurt, angry, or upset, we may need some time to sit in those feelings as we work through them. I believe that our natural state of being is that of peacefulness and love. Yet, sometimes other feelings are so strong that we don't feel very loving. We must go through a process of working through our feelings to eventually get to a place of peace. Venting is one of the tools that we can use to begin to sort through our feelings. Venting helps us release our pent up emotions in a constructive way.

The purpose of venting is to give our feelings a voice and a release valve. When we give our feelings a voice, we are better equipped to move through them, instead of getting stuck in them. Complaining, judging, and blaming keep us repeating the problem without seeking solutions. Venting is a commitment to moving forward. When we vent, we are seeking resolution and closure. We are seeking to release our feelings so that we begin to process the situation more effectively. Venting helps us remove the emotional clutter so that we can access our own inner wisdom and find resolution. Venting is also a way to feel like our feelings are being heard by someone else when we need it most.

Picture a toddler who is having a tantrum because his mother would not let him have an ice cream cone. The toddler keeps repeating over and over that he wants it. He wants it! He wants it and in his eyes, his mother keeps ignoring his request. His mother, of course, may have valid reasons for not wanting her child to have an ice cream at this time. She scolds the child for having a tantrum and decides not to indulge inappropriate behavior. However, because of the toddler's age, he does not fully understand the reasons behind his reality. He just knows he wants that ice cream cone and he does not feel heard. His feelings are so overwhelming that the only thing he knows how to do in that moment is cry and stomp his feet.

He clearly wants a different result. Yet, much of his frustration revolves around the fact that he did not feel heard and his feelings were not acknowledged. He wants someone to say, "I hear you. You want an ice cream cone and I hear that. I understand that you want that ice cream cone. I understand that you are frustrated that you are not getting what you wanted." I use this example for the sake of simplicity. Clearly, as we grow up, we can face much larger challenges. Yet, when we do feel disappointed, angry, or hurt, we may still need some time to work through our feelings about the inability to get what we want.

> *Venting helps us remove the emotional clutter so that we can access our own inner wisdom and find resolution.*

I am a firm believer that we all must take full responsibility for our choices, behaviors, and feelings. Yet, we are not on this planet to move through life alone. Having connection and intimacy with other people is very important to our overall growth and sometimes, we just need to feel like we are being heard. Venting helps us to feel heard. Venting allows us to say that we wanted that ice cream cone! It allows us to express that we are in pain or we are disappointed or we are hurting. We wanted a different result than the one we got and we do not know how to work through our feelings at this moment. We want to let those feelings out and feel heard by someone. We want to feel like somebody is listening. We want to feel like it is ok to be disappointed or frustrated for a while. Remember, the opposite of venting is "stuffing" our feelings down. Denying our feelings will not move us forward. Venting helps us sort through our emotions and look for solutions.

In order to make venting a productive process instead of reverting back to complaining, I want to make some suggestions:

- Choose a person that you trust, other than the person you are angry at, to vent to. As you move through your feelings, you may choose to have a conversation with that person at a later time, but right now, it is time to vent.
- Mutually agree with the person that you are venting to that this is a venting process and during the process, it is a no judgment zone.
- State what you are angry at and what you are feeling. State the outcome that you wanted. Share your disappointment. Let the feelings pour out.

- The ventee's job is to listen and then mirror some of the statements that the ventor makes. For example the ventor might say, "I am angry that John left me. He said he would stay forever. He said we would work through any challenges we had together. He let me down." The ventee would mirror some of the statements made. She might say "I hear you. You are angry that John left you. He said he would work through challenges with you." The ventee is not necessarily agreeing with the ventor's opinion. She is not acting as a judge or placing blame. She is not fixing, rescuing, or taking sides. She is merely *hearing* what the ventor is saying and repeating it back.

- After releasing, you must accept the truth of what is, not what you were hoping it would be. State what the real outcome is. State the reality of the situation.

- State one thing you have gained as a result of facing this situation. What are you learning? What are you grateful for? This exercise begins to shift your thinking toward moving forward.

- State an intention about the situation. What are you committed to doing based on your value system?

- Thank the person you vented to for listening.

After venting, the goal is to get your feelings out, to feel heard, and to find your way back to living by your intentions. For smaller issues, this is entirely possible. You may be able to release it all once and let it go. Bigger issues may take more processing time. You may need to vent again or release your feelings through journaling. Just decide not to revert back to complaining. Remember, venting is a commitment to move forward toward resolution.

The Healing Power of Gratitude

"How can I be grateful that I was in a car accident? How can I be grateful that I got breast cancer?" Carol asked. It can be challenging to find gratitude in some of the greatest difficulties of our lives. Yet, when we are able to shift our thinking, we get more of a sense of closure on the events that bring us pain or sadness. In order to free ourselves from our negative thoughts, we must be willing to see the gifts in every experience. Again, it may take some time to sort through feelings and vent before finding gratitude. This process is not necessarily about being grateful that event happened, but grateful for the by-products of the event. We can be grateful that our family pulled together, that we learned to appreciate each other more, and that we learned about our own strength. Gratitude teaches us to live in the moment and appreciate the here and now. Seeing gifts in every experience shifts our mood and our attitude. The gifts help us heal old wounds and move forward.

Our attitude is a reflection of how we feel about ourselves and the world. Both positive and negative thoughts affect our overall state of being. Our attitude is the outward expression of our internal thoughts and a reflection of how we approach life. If our energy is negative on the inside, it will show itself on the outside through our words and actions. When our approach to life is fear based, we act fearful. We get defensive, blame and accuse. If our inner energy and thinking is positive, it will also show through our words and actions. When we have a positive approach to life, our attitudes and relationships are enhanced and we see the world as filled with wonder. Emerson wrote, "What you are shouts at me so loudly, I cannot hear a word you are saying." The truth of your inner attitude will always show itself.

Derek's Story

Derek had a challenging relationship with his parents. When his parents divorced during his childhood, he felt abandoned by his father and distant from his emotionally guarded mother. In his thirties, he got married, had two beautiful children, and a few years later went through a bitter break up himself. After his divorce, intense feelings of anger, sadness, and loss began to surface. For a while, he went through the motions of surviving and appeared to be moving on. Yet, as he faced challenge after challenge in his personal and professional life, it became apparent that he had some underlying feelings and fears that he had not yet dealt with.

Derek used me as his venting partner. I encouraged him to go ahead and yell through the phone in order to release all of the feelings he had stuffed down. I wanted him to get the rage and the pain out in the open. After our session together, I suggested that Derek continue venting and use a journal to write down all of the emotions that he was feeling. He was angry at his parents. He was angry at his ex-wife. He was angry at himself for not making better choices. Acknowledging his feelings was a great step forward because he had denied them for so long. All of the events that he was angry about had taken place in the past, but they were significantly impacting the way he conducted his life in the present. He wanted his parents to be different than they were. He wanted parents that stayed married, that were loving and connected, and that offered constructive criticism instead of condemnation. He wanted a wife that was supportive and rational, instead of so reactive all of the time. He wished that he had been different: more assertive, more true to himself, and less needy.

Derek's anger began to soften and gave way to feelings of sadness. He felt like he needed to mourn the loss of how he wanted his life to be and learn to accept the reality of the way it really was. He used some of the steps in the forgiveness process and began to feel compassion for himself. As he gave himself compassion, he forgave himself for the moments that he acted out due to his fear. He accepted himself as a human being with human emotions. He could see more clearly that the people in his life were also caught up in their fear. They did not set out to make his life miserable. They were responding in a way that was consistent with their own fears and level of knowledge.

As Derek moved through his feelings, he was more open to see the gifts in his experiences. While his past seemed filled with painful memories, he could find gratitude for some of his experiences. He wrote a letter of gratitude in his journal to his mother, his father, and his ex-wife. The purpose was not to condone their choices or behaviors, but to facilitate his own healing.

He was grateful that his parents had brought him into the world and gave him a chance at life. While he wanted more from them in his childhood, he did learn how to take care of himself and to be independent. He was grateful for that. They gave him a little brother whom he loves dearly. They gave him some wonderful memories: going to his first parade, teaching him to ride a bike, and encouraging him to try out for the baseball team. He started to see that he was grateful for so many moments.

He was grateful to his ex-wife for bringing his two children into the world. He was grateful for the experience of feeling love for as long as it lasted. He was grateful for what he learned from her: how to cook healthy meals, the importance of reaching out to friends, and how to be true to himself when they divorced. Focusing on the gifts in his experiences was actually a gift to himself. It helped him shift his thinking from lack and pain to growth and strength. When he was able to shift his thoughts, he no longer felt burdened by the past. He felt free of it.

Gifts and Gratitudes

There are many ways to shift our thinking from lack to gratitude. The first step is gaining awareness of when we complain and judge. When we catch ourselves complaining or judging, we can turn that thought into something to be grateful for. For example, if I catch myself complaining about the mountains and mountains of laundry that my family creates, I can do a couple of things. I can work on creating a more effective plan to manage the laundry, focusing my energy on a solution instead of the problem. I can also shift my perceptions about my laundry mountain by expressing gratitude. I am grateful that I have a big family with active lives that create lots of laundry. I am grateful that I can do my laundry in the convenience of my home. I am grateful that my ten year old machines continue to work so hard for me. Quite frankly, complaining about the laundry is only going to put a damper on my mood and I would much rather be grateful for the blessings that come with having loads of laundry.

Another way to shift your attitude is to simply write in a Gift and Gratitude Journal everyday. I found this exercise very powerful when I hurt my back. Not only did I enjoy writing what I was grateful for, I enjoyed going back and reading what I had written. Re-reading my journal entries brought those positive feelings back to me instantly. It is a gift that keeps on giving. When I have moments of feeling sorry for myself, as we all do, I write new entries or go back and re-read my old entries. They are uplifting and they support me in returning to my authentic self. Writing "Gifts and Gratitudes" in a journal can truly be life changing. I recommend a couple of key points when writing in a Gratitude Journal:

I am Grateful Today …

- Make your entries specific about the present day or present situation.

- Keep your language positive and focus on what you do have instead of what you do not have; what did happen instead of what did not happen.

- Write about what you truly appreciated about your day. You can also write about how this day enhances your ability to create your future and expand your possibilities. Write about who you appreciated.

- Make your entries as specific and detailed as possible. Notice the sights, textures, smells, and sounds of what you are writing about.

- Write at least three per day. Preferably more. The more gratitude you see, the more your attitude remains positive. It is not possible to stay angry or to feel stressed while writing about gratitude.

As a parent, I have found that asking my children to develop an attitude of gratitude has been an extremely useful tool. Sometimes I say to myself, "I see the abundance all around them. How can they not see it?" Ah, what a lovely reminder that we all are surrounded by abundance. Abundance is not just material things. Abundance is friendships, opportunities, love, hope, and possibilities. When one of my children complains about what is wrong or what they do not have, I often ask them to list, in vivid detail, what they are grateful for right here, right now.

One of my children was in a mood to complain recently. He complained that he could not find matching socks, that he could not go out with his friends, that he had to clean his room, and on and on. I asked him to write 25 Gifts and Gratitudes. We sat down and talked about each item on his list. I asked him to describe each entry in vivid detail. I asked him to tell me every detail about his gratitude for his sister, his brother, his clothes, his room, etc. He looked at me like I had horns growing out of my head, but after he was finished, his attitude had completely transformed. He was back to being the kind, considerate, loving child that I knew he was inside. Gratitudes change attitudes!

When you face a challenging situation, it is especially important to write about the gifts that you will receive as a result of facing the challenge. Think of the things you get to experience, learn, and do as a result of facing a new challenge. I am grateful for this challenge because I am learning patience. I am grateful because I get to practice communicating with my mom in a new way. The challenge may or may not be resolved. It may have been a short term challenge or it may be a long term challenge. The more gifts you can find in the experience, the more you will be able to feel at peace as you move forward. You will feel more empowered to make choices for your life. You will see opportunities instead of problems. I encourage you to write additional entries in your journal around gifts:

> *The more gifts you can find in a challenging experience, the more you will be able to feel at peace as you move forward.*

Gifts

- Write your journal entries focused on a specific challenge.
- Keep your language positive.
- Make your entries as specific and detailed as possible.
- What is the gift in facing this challenge? What do you get to learn? What skills do you get to develop? What opportunities can this challenge help create? Some examples might be: I am grateful for this challenge

because I get to learn how to become more assertive. This is an opportunity for me to practice being true to myself and trusting my instincts. I am growing as a result of this experience.

Reciprocity

As many of us go through life, we think that the "act of giving" causes us to "lose" something. If we give something to another person, we will somehow have less for ourselves. If we praise another person, we will have less power. If we share our expertise, we will be less influential. We see giving to another as giving away a piece of our own worth or importance. I have heard parents say that they are toughening up their children and preparing them to face an unsympathetic world. Or they say, "My parents never complimented me and I turned out ok." Some people are catty instead of supportive. Some see themselves as in continual competition with others. Some people belittle instead of uplift or give a compliment with a little added dig. To me, it is all fear-based bunk.

The truth is when we give from the heart unconditionally, there is a boomerang effect and gifts come back to us. When we give, we end up receiving in ways that are seen and unseen. We feel better about ourselves when we give from our hearts. When we give a compliment, we are acknowledging another person. We are embracing our humanity and their humanity. We are raising the spirits of another person and in turn, raising our own self-esteem. When we offer an unconditional, genuine compliment, we feel good about ourselves while showing care for another person. When we lift others up, we lift ourselves up. Giving a compliment does not take away from us; it gives to us.

Reciprocity is based on the idea that we reap what we sow. In other words, when we choose to take any action that lifts up another person, we lift ourselves. When we help raise the self-esteem of another person, we raise our own self-esteem. When we do something loving, we increase our own self-love. It also works in the opposite way with unconstructive criticism. When we choose to lower the self-esteem of another person through our words or deeds, we lower our own self-esteem. Whatever energy we put out into the world comes back to us.

Giving to others creates a ripple effect like throwing a stone into water. When we give to others, we pass along positive energy and give it direction. The person we give to feels the positive energy and is more inclined to give to another. We have the power to change the energy of the world through our desire to give to others. Acts of kindness create change. I am not talking about being an enabler or helping others avoid personal responsibility. I am talking about uplifting another spirit by being kind or being loving. The gift in giving is receiving a sense of personal pride. Choose to give compliments daily. Make offering random acts of kindness part of your daily routine.

During an average day, how often do you say "thank you"? The more you say it, the more you can shift your thinking to gratitude and abundance. We see a world filled with abundance when we thank others. Good manners aside, it is important to express thanks to others as we move through our day. Again, when we say thank you, we are acknowledging another person and connecting with them. We are appreciating who they are and what they do. We are letting them know that they are valued.

> *The truth is when we give unconditionally, there is a boomerang effect and the gifts come back to us.*

Appreciating Others

- Each day, choose to say or do something kind for another person. Offer sincere thanks for the contribution they have made to your day, to your work, or to your life.
- Write an entry in your journal, "Today, I showed kindness to another person by…
- Note how you felt about yourself.

Living life with an attitude of gratitude is a choice. We can choose to see opportunities in every situation. It is not about pushing feelings down, it is about moving through our feelings to a place of peacefulness and love. Gratitude shifts our focus from lack to abundance. It moves us away from fear, doubt, judgment, and complaining.

Gratitude helps us appreciate the present moment. It helps us become more adaptable to whatever challenges and opportunities that come our way because our frame of mind is positive. Life becomes an adventure filled with hope and enthusiasm. We feel more in control of our life and our choices. We are more open to unplanned opportunities when we are grateful. Every experience we have is an opportunity to celebrate because we are learning, growing our skills, and building our confidence.

Action for Life Exercise

In what area of your life do you find yourself complaining most often?

What are the costs of complaining?

What are the benefits of complaining?

How do your complaints factor into personal responsibility?

What complaints can your turn into requests for change or solution seeking?

What complaints can you turn into gratitude?

How often to do find yourself avoiding giving to someone else in order to preserve your own feelings of worth or power? What could you gain from taking a risk in this area?

If you have recently faced a challenge or are in the midst of facing a challenge, what can you gain from the experience? What do you get to learn? What gifts do you see? What are you grateful for?

How would being kind or loving to someone else today impact your feelings about you?

How can you incorporate random acts of kindness into your daily routine?

How can you show appreciation of another person today?

Create a Gift and Gratitude Journal and make daily entries.

Action for Life Team

Who are your favorite people to complain with?

How can you change these relationships?

Who will support you in releasing complaints?

Who could you vent to?

Chapter Strategy

Stop focusing on what is wrong in your life and in your world. Stop complaining and start focusing on what is right. Seek solutions to challenges and have an attitude of gratitude.

Chapter 7 Key Points

- We tend to either have an optimistic attitude or a pessimistic attitude in specific areas of our life.
- An optimistic attitude opens us up to possibilities.
- The Law of Gratitude helps us to notice what is good and what is working in our life. It shifts us into feelings of abundance.
- Discontent comes from within, even when you think it is about someone or something else.
- Complaining targets problems, not solutions, and prevents us from taking constructive action.
- Complaining focuses on what is wrong and allows fear to stay in control.
- Gratitude focuses on what is right.
- Venting allows us to release our feelings, feel heard, and re-focus on our intentions.
- Seeing the gifts in a challenging situation can facilitate the healing process.
- Gifts and Gratitudes shift our thinking into being thankful for "what is".
- Giving is receiving. Choose to give. Choose to appreciate others. Choose to give thanks.

Chapter 8

Acknowledge Progress and Celebrate Victories.

> *"Once your have tasted flight,*
> *you will forever walk the Earth*
> *with your eyes turned skyward,*
> *for there you have been,*
> *and there you will always long to return."*
> *-Leonardo da Vinci*

"You are such a loser! You are such an idiot. You never do anything right. You screwed up once again. I can't believe you do this kind of stuff over and over again. What in the world is the matter with you? What is your problem? Quit being so lazy! Being tired is not an excuse. What are you thinking?—oh, yeah, you're not thinking. You look like crap today. Nice dark circles. You are getting so fat. Look at this cellulite. Why can't you eat healthy foods? You ate junk food AGAIN! You did not exercise AGAIN! You did not take care of yourself AGAIN! You know exercise is good for you, but are you ever consistent? NO! Why can't you finish what you start? You are so irresponsible. You are so disorganized, when are you going to get your act together? Why don't you take better care of yourself? You know better. You don't have any self-discipline. You must not want all of the things you say you want because you never make the time to do anything. You are full of excuses. You make up justifications instead of being responsible. Why didn't you plan better? You said the wrong thing again. Why don't you make better choices? You are not as good as them. Give it up. You will never achieve your dreams. Your work is not good enough. You should do a better job. You should be able to handle things on your own. Why can't you hold your ground? Why can't you stand up for yourself? It is all your fault. You look like a fool. Why didn't you trust your intuition? You made another stupid decision. You are such a disappointment!" she said.

Pretty harsh language, isn't it? It is downright abusive. Would you ever say these things to someone else? Would you ever, even for a moment, consider talking to your best friend this way? What about your child? If I closed my eyes and envisioned any one of my children's faces, with their big eyes looking up at me, I could never say such horrible things to any one of them. What would be the purpose? To encourage them to do better or be better? To motivate them to achieve? When you read that paragraph, did you find it motivating? If someone was talking to you that way, would you feel excited about embracing new possibilities? It is hard to imagine that anyone could be motivated to change their life, strive for excellence, or reach for their dreams as a result of such critical language. It seems far more likely that the recipient of such venom would desire to seek safety instead of breaking out of their comfort zone.

I am going to be honest and tell you that those words are mine. I have never spoken that way to another soul, but I have spoken that way to myself. I have said every one of those things to me! I have said every one of those things, not once, not twice, but multiple times over the course of my life. When I have done it, I didn't even have to put conscious effort into it. It came naturally. How ridiculous is that? I would never speak that way to another human soul, but I made it acceptable to speak to myself that way. I made it ok to beat myself up emotionally for not living up to a self defined standard. I expected so much of myself and whenever I thought I was falling short, I chastised myself with negative self-talk thinking that somehow it would help me become better. It seems that we all have some form of self-criticism that we believe will motivate us to get moving. Yet, it does not work. I believe that in this case the voice of fear alerts us to some aspect of ourselves that is in need of more self love and nurturing. What do you say to yourself that you would never say to someone else? How motivated do you feel after you do it?

The truth is when we beat ourselves up, it does not propel us forward. It is not motivating. It does not inspire us to reach for our dreams or become our best self. Beating ourselves up and being self-critical in a destructive way erodes our desire to move forward. It diminishes our enthusiasm and our self-esteem. When we beat ourselves up, we are actually perpetuating negative thoughts and feelings instead of inspiring ourselves to action. Our brains believe what we tell ourselves the most often. The more we beat ourselves up, the more we believe that we are damaged, unworthy, or somehow less capable than we really are. Thinking it or saying it to ourselves does not make it true. It does make it destructive, de-motivating, and demeaning.

> *When we beat ourselves up, we are actually perpetuating negative thoughts and feelings instead of inspiring ourselves to action.*

Perfectionism

The Law of Perfection in Chapter 6 states that everything is happening *perfectly* in our lives in order to enable us to learn and grow. Yet, people use the word perfection as a standard to live by. From a transcendental perspective, we are all already perfect. We were born whole and complete with a vast array of gifts within each one of us. Instead of believing that we are already perfect just the way we are, we often use the word *perfect* to describe a standard that is unattainable and unrealistic. We think that perfection is a destination that we can someday achieve, but that place does not exist.

We must either choose to embrace the concept that we are already perfect just the way we are or we must let go of the idea of living in a state of perfection by conventional standards. We often say jokingly, "Nobody's perfect." Yet, deep down inside, so many of us secretly try to achieve perfection anyway. We have an unrealistic belief that if we do everything right, then we will be happy. If we do everything right, our lives will feel complete. If we appear perfect, then we will be more worthy of being loved. People will gravitate to us more and when we have that, we can then show up as our authentic self.

Our thinking is flawed! If we go through life attempting to be perfect and we do receive love, then who is really being loved? The image of perfection we create or our authentic self? People cannot truly love us *as we are* if we choose not to share *who we are*. It is not possible to do everything right because there is no uniform standard of what "right" is. People do not love us more for appearing perfect; people love us for being human and for being ourselves.

We create a measure, or a yardstick, of what we think we should be. We compare ourselves to others. The "others" that we compare to are the ideal, not the typical. We compare ourselves to the most successful, the most attractive, the most intelligent, the most physically fit, the wealthiest… you name it. These are not realistic standards! After we compare ourselves to the ideal and fail to reach those standards, we then judge ourselves for not measuring up. We beat ourselves up and put ourselves down. When we compare ourselves to others, we are not seeing our own unique qualities. We are not seeing our own special gifts or living as our authentic selves. This is perfectionism. Fear is at the heart of it. We begin to think that if we do not portray ourselves as perfect, we will be more vulnerable to rejection, failing, or judgment.

Perfectionism is an effort to not only live up to a certain standard, but also to control everything in our environment. We try to make ourselves appear perfect, our work perfect, and our environment perfect. We are trying to control so many things that are completely out of our control. We are filling our thinking with disempowering and unrealistic expectations of ourselves. The more we seek perfection, the more our stress level rises. We become reactive instead of proactive. The more stressed we are, the more likely it becomes that we will make errors and be imperfect. The reality is that something will go wrong and when it does, we beat ourselves up. We become even more self-critical than we were before. We worry about what people will think. We worry about rejection. It is all fear based thinking. It is a vicious cycle that leads to our emotional destruction. Perfectionism lowers our morale, beats up on our self-esteem, and keeps us stuck in our fear.

Perfectionism is also a desire to portray that we have extensive knowledge and insight. Many perfectionists feel the need to portray to others that they know all of the answers. They want to appear as an expert because it gives them more of a sense of worth. They become "right fighters" who want to be "right" no matter the cost. In their minds, to admit that they are wrong would mean that their worth is diminished.

It becomes important to recognize that no one can know all of the answers all of the time. It is not possible. Letting go of that need to be right is part of letting go of perfectionism. Worth does not change and accepting that you do not know everything is accepting your humanity. Instead of feeling like you must know all of the answers, become a seeker of information. See yourself as an expert *seeker* of information instead of an expert *know- it-all* of information. See yourself as a student in life, someone who wants to continue learning, growing, and evolving. In order to learn, we must choose to be open and teachable.

Being a human being means that we have the power of choice. With the power of choice comes the ability to let our emotions guide our reactions. We may sometimes allow our fears to guide our thinking. We may sometimes make errors in judgment or have misinformation. Part of being a human being is embracing our own humanity. We are here to *learn* to live our best life. There is no destination of perfection that we can achieve. We are already perfect as we are and our purpose is to access our inner gifts. We do that by learning to live as our authentic self and developing our innate skills and gifts. The process of learning and growing creates excellence, not a place of perfection. Excellence is available to any one of us through effort, practice, and commitment.

Here are the keys to releasing perfectionism:

- Accept that a destination of perfection as we define it is impossible and unattainable. We are already perfect as we are and our purpose is to access our inner gifts.
- Stop beating yourself up. Self-criticism is not motivating.
- Accept your own humanity. Be kind and compassionate to yourself.
- See mistakes as an opportunity to learn.
- See life as a journey of learning, growing, and striving for excellence, not perfection.
- Release unrealistic and disempowering expectations.
- Embrace your own gifts and skills without comparing to others.
- See yourself not as an expert in knowing all of the answers, but as an expert in seeking answers and knowledge. Be a student of life. Be teachable.

The Law of Process

When we wake up every morning, our days are filled with tasks and goals that we want to accomplish. We want to accomplish something in our homes, at work, with our families, or for ourselves. Without even thinking about it, we break each goal into smaller pieces that are manageable. For example, if we want our kitchen to look clean, we might first do the dishes, next put the pots and pans away, and lastly, clean off the counter tops. There is a process in everything we do that moves us closer to our goal, no matter what the goal is.

The Law of Process states that in order to achieve a goal, we must decide on a direction, prepare well, and move toward our goal by focusing on each incremental step forward. The reward is not only in achieving the end result; the reward is also in the process itself. With each step forward, we gain knowledge, progress, and momentum. The Law of Process reminds us to savor each step in the journey as if it were an end result in itself. When we acknowledge each success along the way, we are motivated to move forward. When we give ourselves credit and celebrate each step, the reward is in the action itself. As we know, each time we take action, we gain knowledge, build skills, and gain confidence by stretching out of our comfort zone. Simply believing that something can be accomplished opens the door to many possibilities and the Law of Process reminds us that anything can be achieved if we break the journey into incremental steps.

The Law of Process also reminds us that practice is what builds excellence. The more often we practice building a skill, the more skilled we become. Each and every step forward is an opportunity to make an investment in ourself by increasing our experience and building our knowledge level. Sometimes it is important to practice a particular step over and over before moving on to the next step. Practice teaches us patience. Practice creates a strong foundation on which we can continue building upon. If we were building a house, the house is only as sturdy as the foundation upon which it is built. It is important not to rush toward the end goal without taking sure and steady steps along the way. If we skip steps, we are increasing the likelihood that our foundation will not be sturdy. We may need to go back and rebuild.

Additionally, if we focus on only the end result, we may become overwhelmed by the enormity of the work ahead and become paralyzed by fear, unable to take forward action. The most reliable way to achieve any goal is to break it into small, manageable pieces. We must focus only on the task in front of us so that we can create an environment in which we feel capable of handling each individual step. Each step forward is leading us closer to our desired goal. When we follow the Law of Process, we are creating a journey that yields successes each and every day. We are creating an experience that we can feel good about instead of being inclined to beat ourselves up. The journey itself becomes the true reward because we are making forward progress, gaining knowledge and wisdom, and enhancing our own self-esteem and confidence.

> The Law of Process also reminds us that practice is what builds excellence. The more often we practice building a skill, the more skilled we become. The process of taking action becomes the reward in itself.

The Outcome is a Guide, Not a Destination

Having a goal or a desired outcome is important because it sets the course and creates direction. Yet, when we become attached to a specific outcome with no flexibility, we are closing ourselves to possibilities that may arise along our journey. The Law of Process and the Law of Perfection work closely together. The Law of Perfection helps us see that life is happening perfectly to help us gain the knowledge and experience we need in order to live our best life. The Law of Process encourages us to focus on each step, accept the gifts of taking the journey, and then to celebrate each increment of accomplishment.

The outcome is our guide. It helps create direction for the next step forward. It also helps us change course when we are getting off track. The feedback we receive from each incremental step lets us know if we are on track. It helps us review alternative actions and consider new options. It is important to release attachment to a specific outcome because attaching to a specific outcome sets us up for disappointment. We must remember that the true reward lies in the path moving forward. We can view life as a journey with many gifts waiting to surprise us.

Seeing the outcome as a guide is an exercise in releasing control. When we give up control, we give up the need for perfection and are much more open to embracing opportunities as they arise. When we relinquish control of a specific outcome, we are more apt to just go for it and trust that we will gain something for our efforts. We will gain knowledge; we will gain wisdom; we will gain experience; we will gain perspective; and we may even gain gifts beyond our wildest thinking. The only way we can gain anything is by creating an environment, through our thinking, that inspires us to take action.

Acknowledge All of Who You Are

I have noticed with my clients that they can readily tell me what they lack. They can state all of their perceived shortcomings: the knowledge, skills, talents, and attributes that they do not have. They can tell me where they are disorganized, where they feel incompetent, what parts of their body they dislike, when they are impatient, what is wrong with their looks, and on and on. They can tell me all of the things that are imperfect or that are absent. They can tell me all of the things they are not good at. I can tell that they have practiced repeating this because they are so good at it. Most of us are.

When I ask my clients to list what their top 5 strengths or skills are, I often hear long periods of silence. Most people say that they have never even thought about it. They might say something like, "I am nice." What? We are so much more than that and we must learn to give ourselves credit! We must learn to respect ourselves and accept ourselves. We must learn to uncover, love, and embrace all of our gifts. It continues to amaze me that we are all so good at identifying our weaknesses, but sharing our strengths is such a struggle.

The qualities that we admire in other people are often qualities that we have within ourselves. We just are not giving ourselves credit. We compare and think we do not measure up. You might think that someone else is courageous and you deny that you have courage. Yet, you do. You could not recognize courage in someone else if it was not present within you. You might think that someone else has an electric personality, a magnetism that attracts people and still deny it in yourself. Yet, when you show up in the world as your authentic self --loving, whole, and complete-- you shine like a beacon. I know this to be true because I have seen it again and again. We all shine when we give ourselves credit and embrace all of who we are.

While working with one of my clients, he discovered that if he received positive feedback, compliments, and recognition from others, he would perceive the day to be a glorious day. If he did not receive any compliments or recognition, he would feel down and unmotivated. He began to seek more and more attention to feel good about himself. He had become so dependent on the outside world for validation, that he could not create a gratifying day on his own.

When we learn to notice our positive attributes and give ourselves credit, we learn how to create more positive feelings about ourselves. We become less reactive to the opinions of those around us. This is an important component of building self-esteem. We want to be able to feel good about ourselves no matter what anyone else thinks, says, or does. The way we accomplish this is by giving ourselves credit and identifying our positive attributes.

I ask my clients to look at the following chart and circle at least 10 positive attributes or characteristics that they believe they possess. These qualities are a part of our authentic self. What are your top 10 positive attributes?

Positive Attributes

intelligent	accepting	significant	skillful
accountable	silly	supportive	agreeable
leader	artistic	innovative	confident
valued	ambitious	amiable	appreciative
engaging	attentive	authentic	independent
clean	worthy	caring	sensitive
diverse	healing	charming	cheerful
insightful	inventive	clever	brave
giving	self-reliant	reflective	productive
committed	athletic	concerned	hard working
connected	proactive	punctual	reassuring
resilient	relaxed	reliable	motivating
inspiring	secure	powerful	candid
respectful	responsible	dedicated	satisfied
selfless	sensible	sincere	considerate

smart	sociable	centered	conscientious
consistent	determined	positive	strong
content	cooperative	courageous	courteous
creative	curious	honorable	dependable
diligent	disciplined	empathetic	encouraging
resourceful	energetic	commanding	enthusiastic
fair	faithful	self-directed	strategic
flexible	forgiving	focused	friendly
funny	gentle	uplifting	generous
graceful	grateful	happy	helpful
honest	stimulating	hospitable	humble
industrious	joyful	kind	affectionate
loving	loyal	mature	compassionate
neat	modest	observant	optimistic
organized	passionate	patient	peaceful
persistent	playful	expressive	polite
present	principled	unique	supportive
tactful	tenacious	tender	thorough
thoughtful	trustworthy	truthful	understanding
upbeat	versatile	willing	fabulous
wise	calm	stylish	organized
adaptable	analytical	futuristic	positive

Again, this list is meant to inspire you. If you want to add other qualities that you know are part of your authentic self, please feel free to do so. The purpose of identifying our positive attributes is to give ourselves credit and to get in the habit of seeing our gifts instead of focusing on our perceptions of what we lack. Life is so much more motivating when we give ourselves credit.

When I had adrenal exhaustion and spent so much time sleeping, I really beat myself up. The more I beat myself up, the more I sank into the depths of depression. I began to see that my negative self-talk was self-defeating. It made me feel worse about myself instead of better. It de-motivated me instead of inspiring me. I decided to start giving myself credit and celebrating every single step forward, no matter how small or insignificant it seemed at the time. If I found the energy to get up and do the dishes, I congratulated myself. I said, "Kristin, you are awesome. It takes a strong, resilient person to do what you did. Yahoo! Yes! Fantastic!" If I kept my thoughts focused on the task in front of me without beating myself up for being imperfect, I said, "Kristin, today you were focused and persistent. Great job!"

Transitioning from someone who concentrated on being at the top of the sales force to someone who congratulated herself for getting the dishes done felt very uncomfortable for me. My mind wanted to wander back to that place where I expected more achievement from myself. My thoughts wanted to drift back to comparing myself to others and thinking that doing the dishes was nothing extraordinary. Yet, the only way to pull myself from my darkness was to release the past and release unrealistic expectations of myself. The only way I could move forward was to learn to live in the present moment, focus on the task in front of me, and vigorously celebrate each and every step by giving myself credit.

I used a variety of positive attribute descriptors to remind myself of who I really am, under all of the baggage that was weighing me down at the time. Giving myself credit and acknowledging every step forward improved my attitude, my feelings about myself, and brought me closer to my authentic self. Our thoughts are so powerful and our thinking determines whether we see limitations or possibilities. We are 100% responsible for what we say to ourselves about ourselves. This is our choice. We choose what we believe about ourselves.

Sometimes we do not recognize all of the gifts that we each have because we have not yet attempted to access them. For example, imagine asking a child, "Can you roller blade?" The child answers, "I don't know. I have never tried." The child does not know his capabilities, unless and until he has tried. Once he tries, he can better answer that question. He knows his strengths and weaknesses. He knows what he needs to practice to master that skill. It is not a limitation. It is a lack of experience and effort, thus far in his life. He could be a natural or he may need to practice or take lessons, but he cannot assess his skills and talents until he decides to take action. We do not have limitations on what we can become in our lives either. Our only limitations are our thoughts and our efforts thus far.

Skill Sets

After witnessing how few positive attributes my clients could list, I wondered how many of my clients would be able to list their skill sets. As I had anticipated, very few of my clients could rattle off their top skills. Some of them did not think they had any skill sets at all. We all have skills and we all have unique qualities to share with the world. We just do not take the time to identify all of our gifts and greatness. It is critically important to our personal self-esteem to be able to identify our positive attributes and skill sets.

Excellence is a continual commitment to improvement. Athletes practice. Artists, surgeons, and actors practice. Comedians practice. All skills can continue to be improved upon until we achieve a level of mastery. Even then, it often takes effort to maintain a certain level of sharpness and expertise. Personal growth requires work and practice. It is a process. Any time you want to develop and master a skill, you must be willing to invest your time and effort to become better.

Even though you may have room to expand your skills, please embrace, not diminish, the skills that you already have. If you are a parent and you teach your kids how to compromise with each other, then you have conflict resolution skills. If you are great at using your time effectively, then you have time management skills. If you have ever opened a business, you have entrepreneurial skills. I have had clients that say, "I do not have a creative bone in my body." Quite frankly, I don't believe it. Creativity has many faces and we all have creative skills in some form. Creativity can mean that you are artistic, but it can also mean that you think outside of the box and come up with creative ways of approaching a challenge. Our negative perceptions keep us stuck in our limited thinking. We must practice embracing our skills and then building upon them.

Here are some other examples of skills sets that you may have:

selling skills... language skills... facilitation skills... diversity skills...resource utilization skills...problem solving skills... teaching skills... coaching skills... listening skills... speaking skills... networking skills... project execution skills... organizational skills... innovation skills... relationship building skills... writing skills... team building skills... mentoring skills... negotiation skills... interpersonal skills... flexibility skills... communication skills... crisis management skills... leadership skills... service fulfillment skills... visionary skills... motivational skills... management skills... risk assessment skills... process development skills... customer relations skills... capital improvement skills... ergonomic skills... aesthetic skills... order fulfillment skills... talent building skills... stress reduction skills... analytical skills... competence building skills... strategy building skills... adaptability skills.

This is just a snap shot of the vast array of skills that we can learn to embrace and build. The gifts are already within each one of us. It is our responsibility to embrace all that we are and to recognize what gives us a sense of passion. Embracing our skills is not only a gift to ourselves, but a gift to the world around us. When we identify our skills and attributes, we develop more desire to strive toward excellence. More often than not, when we use our natural skills, we feel passion for what we are doing. Passion fuels action. It makes living fun and exciting. Each day ask yourself how you can improve today.

> *Passion fuels action.*

Setting Goals

We have talked about the importance of living by intention in Chapter 4. Intention always contains a verb. Intention is the way in which you want to appear in the world. It is the behaviors that you want to demonstrate. When we set an intention, we are making a commitment to an overall process to do something. We are committing to taking conscious, intentional action. An intention might be, "I am willing to practice acknowledging myself every day." If that is your intention, how would you go about doing that? What would you pay attention to? What would you say to yourself? You would take action steps that are in alignment with your intention practicing giving yourself credit. So, the action steps are actually the goals that you want to achieve in order to demonstrate the behaviors of living by your intention. Let me give another example.

Jenny wanted to lose weight and increase her overall health. She had a target in mind of losing 30 pounds, although she did not feel attached to that specific outcome. She really wanted to feel healthier, have more energy, and fit into her old clothes. Jenny's overall intention was: "I am willing to nurture my body through eating a healthy diet and following an exercise program." Jenny was committing to an overall way of being and she was committing to taking action. If Jenny were to only focus strictly on the goal of losing 30 pounds, she would probably feel overwhelmed by the enormity of the task and become discouraged. She might also become more apt to beating herself up emotionally if she did not live up to her own expectations each day. By focusing on her overall intention, she felt more motivated and she felt like she was setting herself up for success instead of failure.

In order to support her intention, she set goals. She had decided to set daily and weekly goals. Jenny's goals were action steps that supported her overall intention. She had decided that one of her goals would be to eat five reduced calorie mini meals a day. For four of those meals, she wanted to eat one vegetable and she also wanted to have some form of protein at each meal. Jenny wanted to get 45 minutes of aerobic exercise five times per week and do resistance training two times per week.

Her daily goals were:	**Her weekly goals were:**
Eat 5 mini meals per day	Aerobic exercise 5 times
Eat 4 servings of veggies	Resistance training 2 times
Eat 5 servings of protein	Weigh self weekly
Exercise 45 minutes	Take measurements weekly

Jenny's goals supported her overall intention of nurturing her body. If she did not complete every single goal each day, she was still committing to an overall way of being. Her commitment did not change. If she only ate vegetables three days a week, she had not failed. She had merely missed a few of her goals for that week. She was still living by her intention and she was still moving forward.

Jenny felt that in the past, she had not nurtured her body. Deciding to nurture her body, eat vegetables, and exercise regularly were all risks for Jenny. They were risks for her because they were outside her normal patterns of behavior. They were outside of her comfort zone. Every time she took a risk and ate vegetables or exercised, I encouraged her to acknowledge herself and celebrate. She could not focus on any goal that she skipped, only those that she achieved. Through acknowledging herself for every risk and every step forward, she felt more motivated to keep stretching and risking. If she had an "off" day, she was compassionate with herself instead of being self-critical. She was able to stay focused on her intention and eventually created a healthy body and a healthy lifestyle.

An intention is a commitment to a way of being. Goals are action steps that support an overall intention. I suggest that once you decide upon an intention that has meaning to you, create at least one goal each day that will support your intention. Make your goals meaningful. Ask for help from your support team. I also suggest that the goal includes some level of risk or stepping outside of your comfort zone. The only way we grow and build our confidence is by taking risks. Picture your comfort zone as a jail with no walls. If you stay inside, you are living in your own self created prison. If you step out of it, you are free to create the life you really want to live.

> *Embracing our skills is not only a gift to ourselves, but a gift to the world around us.*

Give Yourself Credit

Every time (and I do mean every single time) you take a risk or stretch out of your comfort zone, give yourself credit. Do not measure the size of the risk or compare it to other risks. Simply revel in it and celebrate what you did. If you think a new thought, celebrate it. If you ask for help for the first time, congratulate yourself. If you finally admit that it is your jealousy that hurts your relationships, honor yourself for taking responsibility. If you decided to stand up at a meeting to give your opinion, even though you were afraid and the words barely came out, give yourself credit. If you put your defenses down and showed up as your authentic self, revel in it. If you stop blaming and take responsibility for your life, have a party. Every time you decide to do something differently than you would have done it before, acknowledge yourself. Giving yourself credit is such an important gift to give yourself. It can totally transform how you feel about your life.

Each day, write credits in your journal:

"Today, I give myself credit for: ___"

- Give credits to yourself for any change in behavior or thought. Credits are an acknowledgment that you have risked and stepped outside of your comfort zone.
- State credits in the present. Give yourself credit for what you did today. Do not focus on anything you did not do or did not accomplish. Only focus on what you did do or did achieve.
- Use only positive language. Instead of writing "I did not eat cookies today." write "I chose to eat vegetables instead of cookies."
- Give yourself credit for what you were able to accomplish, the risks you took, and the changes you made. Release any desire to judge the size of the risk. All risks have value and move you forward.
- Be specific and detailed in your entries. You may want to use names, places, or other details that will bring back the feelings of success when you read it later. You can break a larger risk into smaller pieces. For example, you

might give yourself two credits for deciding to go to a social gathering instead of going home and while you were at the social gathering, you initiated conversation with someone new.

- When you take a risk, ask yourself, "What kind of person can do what I just did?" Go back to the list of Positive Attributes and pick a new attribute to recognize within yourself.
- Notice which areas of your life that are the most challenging to give yourself credit. This gives you another tool to notice where fear plays a role in your life.
- Read your credits out loud. Take them in. You earned it.
- As you are preparing to retire in the evening, look at yourself in the mirror and repeat what you have accomplished today.
- Write a minimum of three per day. The more the better!

Credits help us shift our thinking and focus on the positive. They help us access our inner wisdom because they remind us of the truth. In the opening paragraph, I beat myself up with some pretty harsh words. When I am feeling centered, I know very clearly that none of those things I said to myself were true. They are not my truth; those comments were the voice of my fear. Credits help us see all of the amazing things that we are capable of.

A few years ago, I was a brand new speaker, participating in a speaker training program to better my skills, and I was introduced to a corporate meeting planner. She saw me nervously speaking and even making mistakes during the class. After class, I decided to take a risk and ask her if I could meet with her individually one day to talk about my services. She looked me straight in the eyes and said, "Oh, I could never hire you. You are not good enough to speak to my audiences."

At the time, it took so much courage for me to approach her that I was shell shocked by her response and did not know what to say next. I felt so rejected! I wanted to beat myself up and tell myself how stupid I was for approaching her. I stood there frozen for a minute and then I started to hear a voice in my head asking, "What is your truth? What is your truth?" I answered the voice in my head with another thought. "My truth is that I am new, but I am passionate about this topic and my passion helps me give an interesting talk. I have risked and I have grown. I am a good speaker. If I am not a good fit for her, that is fine. I will be a good fit for someone else."

After finding my bearings, I told her that I planned to approach her again down the road equipped with a full portfolio of satisfied customers. (I also thought to myself that my price per talk will probably be higher by then anyway!) Today, my speaking career is in full bloom. Taking risks and giving myself credit has really helped me handle moments like that in a more effective way. It felt like a setback for a moment, but instead of beating myself up, I decided to be kind to myself and focus on my truth. It helped me dust myself off and become motivated to try again.

Lighten Up

The ability to lighten up helps us access our true self. We must be willing to look at each situation from a different perspective. We can take those moments of self-criticism and turn them into an acknowledgement of our truth. For example, instead of calling ourselves lazy, we might look at ourselves from the perspective that we need some rest. We have worked hard and it is time to rest our mind, body, and spirit.

As I was writing this book, there were days when the words just were not coming to me. I felt an urge to be disappointed with myself and beat myself up. I caught myself thinking, "Why can't you get it together and just write?" I stopped that thought and turned it around. Instead I said, "My truth is I have accomplished a great deal in a short amount of time. I feel more creative when I allow myself some down time. Today is the day that I rest." Essentially, we are reframing the negative thought into a positive thought and giving ourselves credit. We are unearthing the truth instead of succumbing to the voice of fear. How can you turn around your negative thoughts?

Experts think that children laugh or smile over 200 times per day on average. Yet, they also say that the amount of smiling and laughing decreases as we age. How often do you smile and laugh? Laughter is a very powerful uplifting force. When we are inclined to beat ourselves up, we can find humor instead. We can see how absurd it is when we try to achieve that non-existent Nirvana of perfection. We can have a sense of humor when things go wrong. Life is so much easier when we choose not to take ourselves so seriously. Laughter increases our energy. It is a physical release for stress and tension. Laughter has even been shown to reduce blood pressure and boost the immune system. It reduces our tendency to create emotional distortions of information. It also lowers our anxiety level by helping us let go of perfectionism and re-focus on our values and commitments. Embrace laughter as much as possible to live your best life!

> *Every time you take a risk and stretch outside of your comfort zone, give yourself credit. Give yourself credit for any new thought, perspective, or action that drives you to grow. Give yourself credit for being the extraordinary person you already are and the person you are becoming.*

Significance

If you were to think about what you want to be remembered for in your life, do you want people to remember you for how good you were at appearing perfect or how much you laughed, loved, and embraced life? Do you want them to remember how often you fought to be right or do you want them to remember how often you made connecting with others a priority? Do you want them to remember that you had perfect hair, a perfect home, and you never admitted to being human or do you want them to remember you for giving love that made a difference in their life? You always have a choice.

In the grand scheme of life, I believe that what we all seek is not success or perfection. We may think we want that, but it is an illusion. What we really want is significance. We want our life to have meaning. We want to feel good about who we are and our contribution to the world around us. There are many, many ways that we each can create a sense of significance. We can develop our skills and share them with the world. We can show up as our authentic self and live fully embracing all of life's possibilities. We can give our unconditional love to others. We can teach others to live a better life by sharing our knowledge and experience. We can offer random acts of kindness and uplift people. We can provide a helping hand or a non-judging heart.

Significance is not about wealth, social status, or societal success. Significance starts with self-love and self-respect. We must first learn to treat ourselves with respect, acceptance, and compassion. We must learn to acknowledge all of who we are and recognize our unique gifts. We must remember that we all have something special to share with the world and our lives are a process of developing those gifts. When we see our lives as a journey or process of growing and becoming our best self, we will then embrace our own significance. Giving ourselves credit is an important part of recognizing our significance. Significance is sharing our unique skills, talents, and authentic self with the world. What brings you a sense of significance?

Action for Life Exercises

When you wake up on the morning, ask yourself the following questions:

What is my intention today? (It may be new or it may be ongoing.)

What risk will I take today? Or what can I do to better myself today?

What skills do I have that I can utilize or what skills do I plan to work on developing today?

If I focused on just one thing that I really like about myself today, what would it be?

How can I give myself credit today?

Are my thoughts motivating me or holding me back?

Think back over the course of your life so far. What successes did you have? What obstacles were you able to overcome? What positive attributes did you possess to be able to accomplish what you accomplished? Get a 3 x 5 card and write all of your positive attributes on it. Carry it with you and every time you feel like beating yourself up, look at your card. Turn your thoughts from self-criticism to self-acknowledgement.

When you are stepping out of your comfort zone and you feel self-doubt, what can you say to yourself to uncover your personal truth and authentic self?

When you feel overwhelmed or stressed by the tasks in front of you, how can you break your tasks into manageable pieces? What would be the first step?

If you felt whole and complete just the way you are, how would that impact your desire to live up to a standard of perfection? How would that impact your habit of comparing to others? How can you simply strive for excellence?

Make a list of your current skills. Keep building upon them. Notice where you feel the most passion. How much of your day is filled with building the skills that you feel most passionate about? How can you use your skills to feel a sense of significance?

Write credits in your journal daily. For each and every step forward, plan to celebrate. Ask yourself, what kind of person can do what I just did? Look at the list of positive attribute descriptors and choose 2-3 descriptors that are reflective of the attributes you have in order to do what you have done. Give yourself credit by acknowledging your positive attributes.

Make up pieces of paper that look like checks. Write a check to yourself every time you risk and take a step forward. See the checks as an investment in the "Bank of You".

What brings you a feeling of significance? What are you doing when you feel this way? How can you use this knowledge in other areas of your life?

Action for Life Team

Who can you ask to help you accomplish your goals? How can they help you?

Who can you turn to when you are facing a roadblock or obstacle? How can they help you?

Who could you read your list of positive attributes to? Are you willing to ask them to identify some of your positive attributes for you?

Chapter Strategy

End negative self-talk, give yourself credit, and celebrate each and every step forward.

Chapter 8 Key Points

- Beating yourself up only serves to reduce self-esteem and reaffirms negative thinking. It is not motivating and it does not inspire you to embrace your potential.

- Perfectionism is fear based thinking. It stems from a desire to feel worth. Strive for excellence instead of perfectionism.

- The Law of Process states that whatever you strive for, you must focus only on the step in front of you. It is each step added together that moves you toward your goals. The gifts of knowledge and wisdom that you gain along the journey are the true rewards.

- Acknowledge your positive attributes. Acknowledge all of who you are.

- Each time you take a step forward, you have a reason to celebrate. No judging or comparing your progress.

- Each step forward enables you to build skills.

- Each time you step outside of your comfort zone, you are taking a risk. Risks help you stand by your intentions and commitments. Goals support intentions.

- Give yourself credit each and every time you take a risk. Write credits in your journal daily. Credits motivate and inspire you. Credits support you in accessing your authentic self.

- Lighten up and stop taking life so seriously. Reframe negatives into positives. Find something to laugh about.

- We all desire a sense of significance. We all want to feel good about ourselves and make a contribution to the world around us.

Chapter 9

Seek to Create Meaningful Communication

"The void created by the failure to communicate is soon filled with poison, drivel, and misrepresentation."--C. Northcote Parkinson

Great communicators have an advantage in this world. Yet, communication skills, like any other skills, are developed, practiced, polished, and mastered. We all have the ability to become great communicators and bridge the gaps of misunderstanding in our relationships. There are six essential components for effective communication: trust, honesty, understanding, commitment, respect, and value. Before I venture into further explanation, I would first like to talk about some of the roadblocks to effective communication. Here is a personal example.

I walked into the kitchen, sighed, and gave my husband the eye roll of discontent. "What is wrong?" asked Rick. "Can't you be a little gentler? You are just jamming the pot into the drawer without putting it in all of the way. Slamming it in there over and over will not make it fit." I said abruptly. "I am not slamming it in there." he responded. "It sure looks and sounds like you are." I said under my breath. To which, he replied, "I can't believe this. You complain that you do not get enough help cleaning up and then you complain about the way I clean up. No matter what I do lately, you are always on my back." From there, our conversation escalated into a full blown argument about the pot. We must have gone back and forth about that silly pot for a good half hour. We fought about what he did, what I did, what I expected, his lack of respect for my kitchen, the way I talked to him, and on and on. Tension had been building in our house for weeks and it all finally blew up over a stainless steel pot.

In the weeks prior, both Rick and I were struggling with our individual issues. I was still recovering from my bout with adrenal exhaustion and I still felt very much weighed down by chronic fatigue. He was sorting through a crisis of his own that was causing him to feel exhausted and drained emotionally. He was worried about his job, being the sole supporter of our family when I left my job, and was also struggling with some chemical imbalances due to his juvenile diabetes. I understood very clearly what he was going through. Although our specific circumstances were different, I understood how overwhelmed by life he was feeling. I had been there before.

As time went on, I noticed a change in myself. Something was brewing within me. I could feel my resentment simmering under the surface, but I had no idea what it was about. I knew I loved my husband and wanted to be there for him. I could completely relate to and empathize with his feelings. I understood his pain and his inner turmoil. There were moments where I felt deep compassion for him and then there were moments where I was downright angry at him. My emotions honestly surprised me. Back then, I was still beating myself up here and there for not feeling what I thought I was supposed to feel. A wife *should* support and love her husband—what kind of person was I to be angry in the middle of his crisis? I stuffed my feelings down for as long as I could trying to be the supportive wife, but my true feelings of resentment were coming out in my daily interactions with him. It all came to a head that day when we began fighting over the kitchen pot.

"Oh my...I just realized that it is not about the pot!" I yelled. "What do you mean it is not about the pot? We have been arguing about this pot for thirty minutes! Of course it is about the pot!" he yelled back. "No, it is not about the pot. It is not about the pot." I said as my eyes filled up with tears. I went in the family room and sat on the couch. He took a few minutes to calm down and then followed me. As the tears streamed down my cheeks, I tried to put all of my feelings into words.

"It is about the pain." I said softly. He tenderly looked at me and let me continue. "I thought I had put the past behind me. I thought I was over all of the pain and shame that I felt when I got sick. My fear kept me on my own hamster wheel, but as I was falling apart physically and emotionally, I felt that you were not there for me. I felt your anger at me about my illness. I knew I was letting you down, but you stormed around and sulked. You made it all about you then and you are making it all about you now. By becoming ill, I knew I was putting more pressure on you to support our family and to take care of the kids. I was sorry that I did that to you, but I did not have a choice because my body rebelled. I was already beating myself up for being stupid, worthless, and incompetent because I could no longer work, be an involved wife, or mother. I was ashamed because my worth was tied to what I could do and all of a sudden, I could no longer do anything except sleep. My darkness was so dark that I would pray that God would take me in the middle of the night while I was sleeping. I had never felt so lost or alone. And you were not there for me. You were angry at all of the pressure I was putting on you. I thought I had put this all behind me and I am surprised that it is coming up now. Here you are struggling in your life and I have done everything I know how to do to be here for you and support you and love you...I feel resentful that I am here for you when you need me and you were not there for me when I needed you the most." It was finally out there, out in the open.

Rick responded, "Knowing what I know now, I feel so sorry that you felt isolated and alone. I was not there for you when you needed me. I was caught in my own fears of being able to support the family, stepping up to take care of the house and kids, and trying to handle my own fear of failing. I was angry and overwhelmed, too. I am so sorry that you went through so much and feeling like no one was there to listen. I understand now and I will be there for you." We had never spoken about it before. I had stuffed so many of my feelings down and never told him what I was really feeling. It felt so good to get it all out. It felt so good to be heard and to be understood. The circumstances of what happened had not changed, but I felt such a sense of healing when he simply listened from a place of empathy and understanding. I was so grateful for the way he talked with me.

After calming down, I realized that I still needed to look deeper within myself. During the prior year when my illness was at its peak, I could have spoken up to share my feelings and I chose not to. I could have asked him for help and I did not. In many ways, he was not there for me because I chose to go it alone. *I* shut him out. I read the frustration in his body language and I chose to internalize the feelings of disappointment instead of talking it out with him. I chose not to communicate with him because of my feelings about myself. When all of the old feelings came rushing back and I said to him, "You made it all about you then and you are making it all about you now", I was still not taking responsibility for my choices. Starting a sentence with "you" was the red warning flag. I was resisting the truth. At the time, I was learning not to be so hard on myself and while I was still in the process of figuring out my feelings, it was easy to move into blaming him and expecting him to be different than he was.

Often when we have a communication break down in our relationships, it is because we get stuck talking about topics instead of the underlying issues. Rick and I fought about the stainless steel pot until it dawned on me that my feelings were not about the pot at all. When our emotions run high, it is easy to slip into patterns of blaming, distorting the facts, and expectations of the other person. We expect the other person to know exactly what we need without speaking up. We get caught up in our own turmoil and forget that other people can get caught up in their fear too. Sometimes we sink into anger, frustration, or sarcasm when we do not feel heard or understood. We become reactive and forget to live by our commitments and intentions. We cannot build the kind of relationships that our heart's desire by choosing inefficient communication tactics. Learning how to communicate effectively is a powerful tool. Understanding the Law of Flexibility is the first step to creating effective communication and meaningful relationships with every one in our lives.

The Law of Flexibility

Every time we have an interaction with another person, we, in effect, are participating in a relationship even if it is only for a few minutes. The Law of Flexibility asks us to actively embrace the truth of whatever arises in the present moment. It essentially tells us to get out of our own way by releasing our resistance and embracing the "here and now". The Law of Flexibility asks us to be accepting of ourselves, of others, of the current circumstances, and of the present moment. It is a waste of our energy and resources to attempt to change that which we cannot change. Life will not always feel fair or just, but we must have the flexibility to adapt to whatever circumstances we are faced with. Only then will we be able to grow and move forward in our lives. The Law does not ask us to be passive or allow ourselves to become victims. It asks us to accept reality and face adversity and good fortune equally.

Picture a large oak tree with many branches. On a sunny day, the branches reach up to the sky, with their leaves glistening in the sunlight. The tree welcomes the sunlight on its leaves and willingly absorbs the sun's energy. On a stormy day, the wind blows the branches of the tree and the branches pull and push, bend forward and back. The branches do not rigidly hold their ground against the blowing wind, but they participate in a fluid dance of flexibility and movement. When we embrace the Law of Flexibility into our lives, we respond to the sun and the storm equally, accepting the reality of what is before us without resisting it. We are willing to bend and to see other perspectives. We are willing to look within ourselves for answers. It is those of us who mentally resist our experiences that feel the most pain, struggle, and inner turmoil. Resistance is the inability to accept the truth of the present moment. Those of us who embrace the truth of *"what is"* are able to utilize our inner wisdom to find solutions, possibilities, and strength. In our relationships, when we remove resistance, we increase connection.

Remove Resistance

Internal resistance is the inability to accept a situation as it is. Internal resistance is focusing on how we think others should be or what we think others should do. It is judgment about how things should be, versus how they really are. Anytime we are not accepting what is, we are focusing on what we perceive to be missing and therefore, creating resistance. We are deflecting personal responsibility for creating our lives and choosing internal conflict. Yes, we are choosing it. We are choosing to bring struggle and discontent into our hearts and minds. The world around us will continue along the same path, regardless of how much we complain about it, judge it, or feel angry about it. Living in denial of what is does not propel us into action or change the circumstances. It keeps us stuck pointing the finger at everyone else. Resistance to the truth keeps us caught in our fear. We want to yell out that life is not fair or that people should be different than they are. We get caught up in holding on to our righteousness and our belief that equality and justice should always prevail. When our relationships are not going the way we want them to, our automatic default becomes, "This is not fair. Life should be fair." When we seek fairness and justice, we are not looking within ourselves. We are looking at the external world and expecting it to be a certain way. This is resistance and this is avoiding taking responsibility for our lives.

Resistance is created within our minds. Since we create internal resistance with our thoughts, resolution can only come about by looking within our own attitudes instead of looking outside of ourselves. We must realize that once again, our perceptions and our fears do not always tell us the truth. We have already talked about the fact that anytime we are angry, frustrated, or irritated, we are harboring an expectation. The same holds true for relationships. Relationships cannot thrive when either person holds on to spoken or unspoken expectations. Expectations and resistance bring up defenses and block true connection.

What do we get when we hold onto our resistance and our desire for emotional justice? We get to feel self-important and smug because we believe that we are right and the other person is wrong. We get to raise ourselves up and feel superior to the other person. They, of course, are not as enlightened as we are, because we are right. We get to blame someone else for the state of the relationship and deflect personal responsibility. We can explain all of our perceived injustices to a third party and get all kinds of pity and sympathy for our plight. We get to live in our excuses because if the other person is not going to do what is right, then we don't feel any obligation to do what is right either. If they are going to act badly, then we are going to choose to act badly as well. We can hold onto our resistance until we feel like we have won. After all, we know we are right and justice is on our side! We believe that our righteousness gives us an excuse to speak with a condescending and sarcastic tone. When we speak down to someone else, we get to feel superior to them, if only for that moment.

It is all resistance and it disconnects us from each other instead of bringing us together. Relationships cannot thrive and communication is ineffective when we are stuck in our patterns of resistance.

> *Resistance is based in fear. It is the inability to accept the reality or the truth of the present moment.*

Action for Life Exercise

How do you interact in your relationships? Think of someone that you have had a disagreement or conflict with. Fill in the blanks:

You make me angry because____.

You should be more____.

If you weren't____, our relationship would be better.

If only you wouldn't____, I would be happier.

You should do____.

It's not my fault. You are making me____.

You make me the victim when you____.

You make me feel ____.

It is not fair when you____.

If you can do ____, then I can too.

When you become more evolved, you will____.

If you were more like me, you would ____.

This is your fault because you ____.

If you weren't so ____, I would like/love you more.

These questions are simply a guide to assist you in creating more personal awareness about what you are really feeling. If you are feeling something that is not listed, please feel free to add it. You may also leave any statement that is not relevant blank. Let's use an example and fill in each statement.

Julia's Story

Julia had an argument with her sister Michelle. Julia said that she understands that she and Michelle are very different, but she wishes Michelle would stop interfering in her life. She wants Michelle to change so that they can have a better relationship. Julia filled in the following:

You make me angry, Michelle, because you try to run my life and you are always telling me what to do. You should be more supportive. If you weren't so critical, our relationship would be better. If only you wouldn't be so bossy, I would be happier. You should mind your own business. It is not my fault. You are making me angry at you because of your actions. You make me feel like the victim when you belittle me for my choices. You make me feel stupid. It is not fair when you come to my home and tell me how to live my life. If you can be a judgmental jerk, then I can too. When you become more evolved, you will figure out that I am far more competent than you give me credit for. If you were more like me, you would see that I spend my time focusing on my family instead of my house. This problem in our relationship is your fault because you don't listen to a word I say. If you weren't so judgmental, I would love you more.

From this exercise, we really have no idea who is right and who is wrong. Rightness does not matter. What matters is that Julia is carrying around inner turmoil. She wants Michelle to be different and she wants their relationship to be different. Yet, she cannot control what Michelle says, thinks, or does. Julia can only control her own thoughts, actions, and emotions. Clearly, she wants to feel differently than she is feeling right now. She cannot change her feelings while she is looking outside of herself and desiring Michelle to be the one who changes.

> *We cannot change our feelings about a situation while looking outside of ourselves and wanting the other person to change.*

Here is part of our coaching dialogue:

Kristin: Is it all true or are you building evidence to justify your thinking? Can you absolutely, positively be 100% certain that if Michelle were not bossy, that your relationship would be better? Can you be certain that if Michelle changed that you would not feel stupid or victimized?

Julia: Well, not exactly, but I am sure that our relationship would improve some.

Kristin: What happens to you by believing that Michelle should be the one to change?

Julia: I guess it makes me feel better, that there is not something wrong with me. The problem is hers.

Kristin: How does this help you get closer to your goal of having a better relationship?

Julia: It doesn't.

Kristin: What hurts or angers you the most?

Julia: I feel judged, belittled, and incompetent when she talks to me. She tells me my house is messy and disorganized. She picks on the way I cook. She says I should find a different job.

Kristin: Is what she saying true or not true? What is your truth?

Julia: My truth is that I do the best I can. I value time with my family and they are my priority. I am tired and overwhelmed. I can barely keep up with my life. I complain about my job fairly often. My house is messy, but I don't need her coming over and reminding me of that. She should just keep her mouth shut.

Kristin: What would happen if you could no longer decide what Michelle should do? If you took away all of your thoughts of judgment about how she should be different, what thoughts are you left with?

Julia: I would think about what I should do.

Kristin: Would you think about what you should do or what you want to do?

Julia: I would think about what I want to do.

Kristin: What do you want to do?

Julia: I want to make changes in how I live my life. I want to learn how to let go of my own judgments and communicate my needs to Michelle.

Kristin: So initially, you were angry at her judgments. How do you feel about *your* judgments?

Julia: I can't believe it. I am judging her and I am judging myself. I am afraid to feel judged by her, but I am judging too by believing that she should be different than she is.

Kristin: What do you mean by "afraid to feel judged"? What is your fear?

Julia: That I am not good enough.

Kristin: Who decides that?

Julia: I do.

Kristin: Tell me about not being good enough.

Julia: (She takes a long pause and her voice quivers.) I am doing my best, but sometimes my best does not feel good enough. I think I should be able to handle life better. She seems to remind me of my shortcomings. I let her give me her opinions and I just get defensive. I don't ask her to change the way she interacts with me. I really do love her though.

Kristin: What do you think your defensiveness reveals?

Julia: It reveals that *I* don't feel good about some of my choices and the way I participate in my life.

Kristin: So, if *you* were different...If you chose not to judge yourself...If you chose not to judge her...If you stood up and asked for what you wanted, what would happen to your feelings in this relationship?

Julia: I would not have this inner turmoil. I would feel more secure about myself when she talks to me. I would ask her to speak to me differently. I would enforce some boundaries. I would let her know how I feel. I would give myself credit for the things I get done. I would make changes in my life. I see now that I am creating this. I can feel more peaceful by taking charge of my life.

How would your relationships change if you did not complain, blame, or judge? If you were incapable of thinking those thoughts, *who would you become and what would you do*? If you were incapable of focusing on what you perceive to be missing, absent, or wrong with someone else, what would you think instead? What would you think if you could only focus on you? What would you think if you were only able to focus on the reality of what is right in front of you in any given moment? In other words, what would you think if you were totally accepting of yourself, others, and the circumstances of this moment? What would you see if you shifted your point of view from outside of yourself to a perspective of complete responsibility for creating your life?

How are your judgments really a reflection of your needs? Is it possible that, in fact, everything is happening perfectly for your greatest good? Is it possible that you are expecting the other person to live by your rule book? Is it possible that building evidence is fear's way of keeping you safe from having to take responsibility for your own life? Is it possible that you are not communicating your needs or living with intention? Is it possible that it is you who must change your perceptions in order to find inner peace?

Typically, when we judge someone else, the very thing that we judge them for, we need to give to ourselves. When we do not feel valued by others, it is a clue that we do not value ourselves completely. When we do not feel loved by others, it is a clue that we do not love ourselves unconditionally. When we judge someone else for behaviors that we do not like, chances are we need to look within and see where we use those behaviors. Are we really being honest with ourselves by defending our judgments or do we really need to get real and look inside ourselves?

If someone judges us, their behaviors and choices may or may not be inappropriate, but by holding on to our resistance, we are giving all of our power to them. We must look within to discover how to stay centered, consider our options, and make choices that empower us to live authentically. We can only control our responses and actions. The more anyone acts out or judges, the more in need they are of their own internal healing. People who judge others are often harboring their own fears and negative self beliefs.

There is an opportunity to gain wisdom in every experience, whether the experience is painful or joyful. Internal resistance comes from within and is always a call to action to look at ourselves. Every time we feel judgment about what the other person should or should not be doing, we must be willing to look inward at our own actions and feelings. We must decide to accept the reality of the present and choose how we are going to handle our own thoughts, feelings, and actions. We must decide whether or not we are going to be a victim of our feelings or we are going to take action to change our perspective. Resistance is a barrier to connection. We enhance our relationships, not by blaming and judging, but by giving up our resistance, accepting the truth of what is, and proactively making choices that release us from our emotional struggle.

> *We enhance our relationships, not by blaming and judging, but by giving up our resistance, accepting the truth of what is, and proactively making choices that release us from our emotional struggle.*

Look Within

Let's go back and look at the statements we made above. From my experience, I can say that it is often challenging to look within when someone else is not holding up their end of the bargain, acts out inappropriately, or brings up hurtful feelings. By looking within, we are not necessarily agreeing with their behaviors or letting them off of the hook. We are choosing to stay centered and look for resolution. We are moving through our feelings instead of staying stuck in them.

Our answers always lie within. The resolution might be simply to trust our own worth and value our opinions. The resolution may lie in negotiating a compromise or it might require standing up for our needs. It might be changing our perceptions and looking at the situation in a new way. It might be letting go of being right and instead, asking for help. The only way we can truly take charge of our lives and create the life we are meant to live is by looking within and then taking action in a way that supports our own needs and self-esteem. Let's begin to change our thoughts by looking inside instead of outside of ourselves.

You make me angry because____.

Anger announces that I am having expectations. I am expecting____. Instead of expecting, I choose to show responsibility for my life by____.

You should be more____.

The outcome I really want in this situation is____. How can I facilitate that happening?

If you weren't____, our relationship would be better.

I am willing to be responsible for my participation in our relationship. I am willing to____ in order to enhance our relationship.

If only you wouldn't____, I would be happier.

How can I ask for what I want? It would really help me if you could____.

You should do____.

I choose to do____ in order to make progress here.

It's not my fault. You are making me____.

By choosing to get upset, I am making me____.

You make me the victim when you____.

I am in charge of my life. I am making a new choice to do____ so that I don't feel victimized. I choose to take care of myself in an empowering way by____.

You make me feel____.

When you do____, I am choosing to feel____ because I am reacting. When I am proactive and choose to live by my intentions and commitments, my feeling becomes____.

It is not fair when you____.

I would rather that you____.

If you can do____, then I can too.

I choose my behaviors, no matter what you do. I choose to do____ in order to stay aligned with my integrity.

When you become more evolved, you will say/do____.

This situation will help me evolve because I will learn____.

If you were more like me, you would____.

I acknowledge my needs and I express them constructively by____.

This is your fault because you____.

In order to be fully responsible for my life, I must say/do____.

If you weren't so ____, I would like/love you more.

I feel better about myself when I say/do____. This supports me in feeling better about my relationships.

Once we look within, we can shift our focus from blame, accusation, and judgment to beginning the process of connecting to others in a productive way.

Conditions for Meaningful Communication

What creates effective communication especially when emotions are involved and finding resolution is critically important? What we really want to do is let love, not fear guide us, even in business situations. One of the coolest descriptions I have ever heard coined is in Tim Sanders' 2002 book *Love is the Killer App:* "Over and over I have discovered that the people in the bizworld, who are the most successful, and the happiest, are the lovecats…They are the ones who are most generous with their knowledge, their address book, and their compassion." "Lovecats" are people who act in a loving way towards others in every relationship. "Lovecats" want to see other people reach their potential and by selflessly promoting others, they increase their own happiness and sense of purpose.

To me, being a "lovecat" is being authentic. Our authentic self is our loving self. Being authentic is showing up as who we really are without our fears shaping the way we interact with others. Imagine how all of our relationships could be enhanced if our words and actions were based in love instead of fear. We cannot control how every person responds to us, but what would happen if we chose to do our best to make sure that the people in our lives leave every interaction or conversation feeling good about who they are as human beings? Imagine how our relationships would change if fear did not affect the way we interact with one another.

There are six principles that are essential for creating meaningful communication, whether it is in a personal or professional relationship. Part of being human, is having needs. People have a wide variety of needs. The most basic needs are food, water, shelter, and physical safety. We also have emotional needs. Whether or not our needs are being met often determines whether the relationship grows or falters. Since we each have a different personal history, our individual needs will vary. Yet, there seem to be six crucial parameters that must be present in relationships in order for the relationship to be beneficial for all parties involved. These are human needs that we all desire on some level. In our relationships, we all desire to feel a sense of: trust, honesty, understanding, commitment, value, and respect. When any one of these parameters is not met within a relationship or conversation, there is a very strong chance of misunderstanding, mist-trust, and disharmony.

> *To me, being a "lovecat" is being authentic. Our authentic self is our loving self. Being authentic is showing up as who we really are without our fears shaping the way we interact with others.*

1. Trust

One parameter that is critically important to creating effective communication is trust. The essence of trust is nurturing a sense of safety in the relationship. It is a reliance on faith that each party will be responsible for choosing constructive words and actions; each party will choose to be open and forthright; and each party will choose to protect the sanctity of the relationship. If any party is hiding their true thoughts, feelings, opinions, or needs, because of a perceived lack of safety, the communication cannot move forward in an effective way. Each person must commit to remove any inclination to blame, judge, or accuse. Blaming and judging will immediately shut down any open lines of communication. Remember that blaming, judging, and accusing are all fear based actions. Each person must commit to making the communication a "no judgment zone". This fosters an environment of unconditional safety.

In order to nurture trust, communicate your thoughts from an "I" perspective. In other words, refrain from saying "you" when developing dialogue. Starting sentences with "you" often feels very accusatory to the other person. Phrases like "You did, you said, you made me..." deflect the focus back to the other person and often initiate defensiveness, breaking down communication. Instead, use phrases that begin with "I". Open your dialogue with phrases like "I think, I feel, I want, or I need" and then continue. This lets the other person know where you are coming from without making assumptions or accusations. Depending on the relationship and circumstance, you can even take it a step farther and incorporate your feelings into the dialogue.

When we feel safe, we are much more apt to share our true feelings and thoughts in a way that gets the real issues out in the open. Trust creates safety and safety creates an opportunity for genuine honesty.

2. Honesty

Honesty is a willingness to be emotionally transparent. It is a willingness to be authentic and open. Emotional transparency requires that each person remove any personal barriers to both speaking and hearing honest opinions and feelings. In every interaction, we make a choice to show up authentically or to show up barricaded behind protective walls built by our fear. Emotional transparency invites us to be willing to let our emotions become visible instead of hidden by our social masks. It helps us detach from our hypersensitivities to criticism and it enhances our ability to communicate openly.

Most of us have had the thought that we do not want to be honest because if we were honest, we would hurt someone else's feelings. Such thoughts are a significant barrier to connection. If you are scared to hurt someone's feelings by being honest, you are really fooling yourself. The reality is that you are either trying to protect *yourself* from feeling uncomfortable by sharing openly or you think that your words are so powerful that someone else will crumble and fall apart if they hear your opinions. If you are withholding honesty because it is uncomfortable for you to speak up, you are choosing to limit yourself and your relationships by staying safe inside your comfort zone. If you choose not to speak up because you do not believe the other person can handle it, you are probably over inflating your power. Either way, effective communication cannot take place without honesty.

I will admit that I was one of those people that kept my thoughts to myself for fear of hurting someone else. As I was learning to coach, I was uncomfortable interrupting a client in the middle of a story. I was very worried about making sure the client felt heard. Overall, listening is an important coaching quality. However, the word "worried" was a clue that I was acting from a place of fear. In order to coach effectively, I needed to learn that interrupting a client that is stuck in their story or personal struggle is essential to their overall growth. I cannot be an effective coach while I am worried about hurting feelings. It is my responsibility to be honest about what I am hearing and to ask questions in a constructive way.

In every relationship, honesty is critical to establishing a meaningful connection. I am not suggesting that you sling mud or blurt out condescending criticism under the guise of honesty. I am talking about sharing from your heart and sharing the feelings that are an integral part of the interaction.

In a business relationship, you might say "I felt confused when you offered the project to Stan. Can you help me understand how you made that decision?" You are speaking from the first person and you are sharing honestly.

In a personal situation, instead of accusing your mate of being inconsiderate, you might say "I felt ignored when you did not introduce me to your friends. I really want to understand where you are coming from." Emotional transparency is speaking from your heart, no matter what your heart is saying. If your best friend has fallen in love and no longer seems to have time for you, speak from your heart. You might say, "I am really happy for you, but I am also afraid our friendship will change. Your friendship means a great deal to me and I want to make sure we find a way to stay connected." Emotional transparency and honesty increases the connection in every relationship.

3. Understanding

Understanding is another condition critical to the quality of communication. Understanding is being open to gaining insight into the thoughts or feelings of another person. We all seek to feel understood on some level. After all, this is why we communicate. We want someone else to be to open to taking in what we have to say.

Part of understanding is accepting others at face value. We do not necessarily have to agree with the opinions of others, but we must be willing to accept them for who they are if we want to have meaningful communication. We accept others for who they are by eliminating our own thoughts of resistance and by using our hearts to create connection. We always have a choice in how we choose to interact. Choosing to enter into an interaction from a place of thoughtful intent and pure motive is the most effective way to create understanding. It is important to understand that other people may have different information filters, a different history, and a different point of reference than we do. Because we are all different, a desire to understand through empathy can be a powerful tool for connection.

Empathy is vicariously considering where someone else is coming from almost as if we could put ourselves in their situation. When we approach someone else through a position of empathy, we become much more open to communicating authentically and relating to what the other person is conveying. Relating creates commonality and commonality creates a connection upon which communication can constructively take place. Commonality can be a shared goal, a shared need, or a shared perspective. For example, if I have a disagreement with my husband, I may disagree with him about the current topic, but our commonality is that we are both committed to working through the issues we face in our marriage. Commonality could also be that we both have the need to feel heard in the heat of the moment. After we listen to each other and both of us feel heard, we may then agree to disagree. When we relate to each other and we share something in common, we are much more willing to keep an open mind.

Let's say that you share a workspace with another person. You like organization and a sense of quiet while you work at your desk. Your work partner, Joe, is an outgoing guy, who zips in and out of the office like a walking tornado. He is loud, somewhat messy, and always in a hurry. Every time he comes into the office to check his messages, he puts his voice mail on speaker phone at a high volume level so that he can multitask while listening to his messages. It totally disrupts your train of thought when Joe does this. What are you going to do? You have a multitude of choices. You can stew silently and curse him under your breath; you can share your position with him and ask for what you want; or you can express your frustration by picking a fight because you think he is so inconsiderate.

Let's say you snap at him and tell him you are tired of listening to his loud voice mail messages and looking at his mess. Chances are Joe will feel defensive with that approach. He may make some changes, but he will resent you for the way you handled the situation. Or he may turn up the volume one more notch just to tick you off some more and watch you squirm. Verbal attacks, while enticing sometimes, do not get us the results that we seek. It is important to ask ourselves, "What do I really want in this situation?" You probably want him to keep his area a little neater and you want him to pick up the hand set instead of using the speaker phone. The most effective way of handling the situation is choosing the path that will most likely get you the results you seek instead of reacting to your emotions.

How could you show empathy for Joe's position while still asking for what you want? A good place to start might be to acknowledge something that you have noticed about Joe. You might say, "Joe, I see that you are working hard and I see that you are attempting to multitask when you are listening to your messages." By showing recognition of Joe's situation, you have shown empathy. Once you show empathy and relate to Joe on a personal level, he is far less likely to respond defensively. Then, it is time to ask for what you want. You might say, "I really work better, when it is quiet. How can we work together in order to meet both of our needs?" You can make suggestions and you can also be open to Joe's suggestions, until you come to a mutual agreement. Through this approach, both of you will feel like you can negotiate seeking a shared goal.

While asking for what you want, make sure to share the relevancy and value of your request. In other words, you are not asking Joe to make changes in his behavior just because you want to be a nit-picking nag and control his every move. You are asking Joe to make changes because of a need. You do not necessarily owe Joe an explanation for your request. You are making a choice to develop commonality and understanding. You convey your need, a need for quiet, and the relevancy of your need, because it helps you work more efficiently. This helps Joe gain empathy and understanding for your position. Mutual empathy and understanding are the foundation of meaningful communication.

4. Commitment

Commitment means that each person is fully engaged in the interaction. Each person is committed to focusing on the conversation with no distractions or excuses. Commitment is intentional participation, including being open to negotiation and actively listening. When we are committed to an interaction, we are completely in the present moment and our body language reflects our dedication to being fully engaged. We face the person we are speaking with and make eye contact. We also commit to listening without interrupting or cutting someone off. We may nod as an acknowledgement that we are listening and we may mirror what we have heard by repeating some of the speaker's words. We are not necessarily agreeing, we are acknowledging that we are listening. We are acknowledging a mutual commitment to seeking a resolution, a solution, or an agreement.

Commitment is also entering into an agreement to discuss a specific topic. Conversations can only move forward when all parties understand the purpose of the interaction. Sometimes, especially when it is an uncomfortable conversation, it is important to mutually agree on a time and place to discuss a touchy subject. Clearly state the issue to inform the other person of the subject. Let them know that you are seeking clarity, negotiation, or resolution. Ask for a time that would work for both of you. By setting up a specific time, all parties have the opportunity to decide what parameters are most important to communicate or resolve. There is also less chance that emotions will drive the conversation.

I have several memories of commitment break down when I was in sales. Most of my work was by appointment, so my customer and I had entered into an agreement to discuss my product during our allotted time together. I really enjoyed it when my customers were active participants in my presentation and asked questions. The situations that were most frustrating for me were the times when a customer would say, "Just tell me about your product and I will listen." It sounded good at first, but I quickly learned that those customers were the ones that mentally checked out of the conversation. I would start to share my information, and they would look down at their desks, shuffle through papers, or constantly answer the phone. I even had one customer that sat there and cut his nails while I was in the middle of my product presentation! Eeew! Having experienced a few of those situations, I learned to stop speaking until they looked up at me or I initiated questions to re-engage them. As my skills grew, I became more confident in seeing our equal worth and expressing that my time was as important as theirs while still being respectful.

5. Respect

Respect is another condition that is important in creating effective communication. There is not a person on this planet that does not want to be treated with dignity and respect. Yet, when emotions drive the interaction, respect is often the first parameter to go. Respect is demonstrating regard for the other person's thoughts, feelings, and opinions. It is also treating others as having equal worth. Their feelings have equal value to your feelings. Their needs have equal value to your needs. Their worth equals your worth. Respect requires that we see each other as competent and capable. We speak to each other with appropriate language and voice inflection. No talking down or making derogatory comments. When we treat someone else with respect, we are acting in alignment with our own integrity. When we are disrespectful, not only do we break down the lines of communication, we damage our own self-esteem piece by piece. Yelling disrespectfully or name calling, may feel powerful in the moment, but it ultimately weakens us from the inside out.

Showing respect is also sticking to the point of the conversation at hand instead of bringing up past mistakes in order to humiliate someone else. We have all made mistakes and bringing up past mistakes serves no purpose.

Showing respect also means separating the person from the behavior. For example, I might not have liked a choice that my children made, but I love and respect who they are unconditionally. I can speak about the behavior, not the person, while still communicating my thoughts in a respectful way. Respect is reciprocal. The more we show respect for ourselves and others, the more we receive respect.

How we engage in disagreements determines how successful our relationships will be. If we are committed to resolution while treating each other with respect, there is a strong chance for a successful relationship. If we digress into disrespectful behavior, the relationship tends to be doomed. Disrespect fosters anger, resentment, and dissatisfaction. Character assassination will not move the relationship forward. There is never a valid reason to act disrespectfully toward another human being. No matter who we are interacting with, we must commit to communicating in a way that shows respect and preserves the other person's self-esteem.

> *Respect is reciprocal. The more we show respect for ourselves and others, the more we receive respect.*

6. Value

Value is the final essential component to effective relationships. We have already touched on the fact that most people truly desire a sense of significance in their lives. We want to feel like we are making an important contribution to the world. The same goes for our interactions with other people. We all want to feel a sense of significance. We want to feel like our thoughts, feelings, and opinions count. We want to feel as if we matter and our contributions are appreciated. The most productive relationships are those where people feel as if they have significance. Feeling a sense of value inspires loyalty and commitment to the relationship.

Value transcends the situation. Whether the relationship is personal or professional, we all want to feel like we are valued. We can show that we value someone by demonstrating appreciation for who they are or how they contribute to the relationship. Give a compliment. Acknowledge their gifts. Give credit where credit is due. Say thank you. Say, "I value you because…" Offer a random act of kindness. These are all ways to express value.

Effective Communication Principles

❖ Release resistance and accept *what is*.

❖ Communicate from a place of integrity, intention, and commitment, not emotional reactivity.

❖ Acknowledge your feelings while still acting on your intentions.

❖ Agree to communicate in a "no judgment zone" in order to establish trust and safety.

❖ Enter into the conversation being willing to be honest and emotionally transparent.

❖ Get clear on what you want to accomplish through the conversation.

- ❖ Acknowledge the other person's situation with empathy. If you are not clear on their situation, ask questions about their perspectives and needs.
    - I can see that you____.
    - I understand that you____.
    - What are your needs here?

- ❖ Seek to relate or find something in common. Seek common ground. Speak with inclusion, not isolation.
    - We both want ____.
    - We have ____ in common.

- ❖ Use a respectful tone and language.

- ❖ Remember that typically when we speak, whatever we put out there comes back to us. If we speak respectfully to someone else, we receive respect back. If we speak with anger, we receive anger back.

- ❖ Accept that all parties have equal worth and each person's needs have equal value.

- ❖ Commit to engaging fully and actively listening. Make eye contact. Intermittently acknowledge what you have heard by mirroring the words that the other person has said.

- ❖ When speaking, speak from an "I" perspective
    - I want____.
    - I think____.
    - I feel____.

- I need____.

❖ Share your feelings in order to increase understanding. You might say:
  - I felt angry when____.
  - I felt hurt that____.
  - I felt upset because____.
  - I felt disappointed when____.
  - I felt unimportant when____.

❖ Watch for the use of "you". This is usually a sign of placing blame on the other person. Be willing to look within.

❖ If there is a misunderstanding, take responsibility for your role in it. If there is a reason for you to apologize, then do so.
  - I am sorry that I____.
  - I recognize that I did____.
  - It was not my intention to____ and I apologize.
  - My approach could have been better. I will work on____.
  - I take responsibility for____.

❖ Ask clarifying questions.
  - What do you mean when you say____?
  - If I understand, you are saying that____.
  - Can you tell me more about____?

- ❖ Ask for what you want while being open to a dialogue of negotiation and alternate actions.
    - What do you need in order to feel better about this situation?
    - In order to feel more____, I would like to see____ happen.
    - How can we work together to come to a compromise?
    - What would work better for both of us?
    - Let's brainstorm some alternative actions.
    - Next time, can we____?
    - In the future, I would like to____.
    - Next time, it would help me out if____.
    - That is a good idea and I would like to add ____.

- ❖ Reveal the value and relevancy of your request.
    - I would appreciate it if you would do____ because I feel/need____.
    - This is important to me because____.

- ❖ In certain situations, a timeline may be appropriate.
    - When can I count on you to follow through?
    - When will we initiate our agreement?
    - How much time do you need?

- ❖ In certain situations, a written agreement may be appropriate. This may reinforce each person's commitment to the agreement.

- ❖ Show appreciation for the other person. Let them know what you appreciate about them.

- ❖ Thank the other person for their commitment to resolution.

Action for Life Exercises

What are you expecting someone else to do in the relationship?

What hurts or angers you the most?

What is your truth?

What would you think about if you could no longer focus on anyone except you?

What would you decide to do differently?

How can you shift your resistance to acceptance?

How could acceptance create more serenity in your life?

How can you create more effective communication?

Practice spending one entire day with the intention of uplifting, promoting, or acting loving towards every single person you come into contact with. Notice what changes in your life.

Action for Life Team

If you are facing a challenging conversation, who can you ask to practice with you?

Who can you trust to give you feedback on your communication approach?

Chapter Strategy

Remove resistance in communication, accept the reality of *what is*, speak from "I", and meaningful communication will grow.

Chapter 9 Key Points

- We often have disagreements about topics, when in reality we must address the underlying issues.

- The Law of Flexibility asks us to accept ourselves, accept others, accept our current circumstances, and face adversity and good fortune equally.

- Internal resistance is focusing on how we think things should be instead of the way they really are.

- Internal resistance is created by our thoughts. We create our own suffering and inner turmoil by refusing to accept *what is*.

- Life will not always seem fair or just. We get in our own way when we attach to fairness. We must choose to be flexible and accept the truth of whatever comes our way.

- Choose to be a "lovecat" in every aspect of your life.

- There are 6 essential components for effective communication: trust, honesty, understanding, commitment, respect, and value.

- Trust is creating a sense of safety for each participant in the conversation. Trust is creating a "no judgment zone".

- Honesty is the willingness to be emotionally transparent, authentic, and open.

- The inability to be honest reveals that you cannot face your own feelings of discomfort or you think that you have so much power that other people cannot handle your thoughts. Either way, it creates communication barriers.

- Understanding is offering empathy. It is being willing to consider where the other person is coming from.

- Commitment is being fully engaged in the conversation by using eye contact and active listening. It is staying in the present moment without dredging up the past.
- Respect is demonstrating regard for another person's thoughts, feelings, and opinions. Respect is viewing each person as having equal worth. My worth equals your worth. My needs are as important as your needs.
- Value is showing appreciation and embracing the contributions that each person makes to the communication process and to the relationship.

Chapter 10

Attract What You Want with the Right Mindset

"See the things that you want as already yours.
Know that they will come to you at need.
Then let them come. Don't fret and worry about them.
Don't think about your lack of them.
Think of them as yours,
as belonging to you,
as already in your possession."
--Robert Collier

As we begin to master our fears and utilize the tools in this book, our thinking will shift. With new thoughts come new opportunities for abundance. Life is filled with possibility and opportunity when we choose to be open to it. Our thoughts and beliefs can create a powerful self-fulfilling prophecy. When our thoughts are preoccupied with lack, pessimism, and judgment, we receive lack, pessimism and judgment in our lives. When our thoughts generate positive energy, love, acceptance, and abundance, we in turn, receive the gifts of love, acceptance, and abundance.

The Law of Abundance

I view the quote by Robert Collier on the previous page as an example of how affirmations support positive thinking and attraction. The Law of Abundance states that we can draw the energy of abundance and success into our lives by first creating visualizations of success in our minds. If we can see it first, with vivid detail in our minds, we can create it in our reality. Abundance does not just refer to possessions or money. Abundance can be love, friendship, spiritual evolution or any of a variety of needs and desires.

In order to utilize the Law of Abundance, we must have a mindset of balance. In order to receive abundance, we must believe that it is possible and we must be open to receiving it. Once we are willing to receive gifts of abundance, we must also be willing to give back to the world with equal compensation. We can give knowledge, time, love, or offer reciprocity in other forms.

Visualizations are affirmations of our belief in our possibilities. So, anything we desire, we must first be able to see it as already ours in our minds. You may be thinking that you are not the kind of person that can visualize. As you are reading this, visualize yourself walking into your kitchen, going to the cupboard, and reaching for a glass cup. See your hand grasping the cup and laying it on the counter top. Now, see yourself walking to your refrigerator and pulling out a bottle of cold water. Pour the water into the cup. Hear the echoing sound of the water filling the cup. Feel the cold on your hand as the condensation starts to build on the outside of the glass. Bring the cup to your lips and feel your thirst being quenched. You just created a visualization.

It is easy to visualize pouring water into a cup because you have done it before. Yet, we can also visualize new events in our minds with the same vivid detail. Picture yourself driving down the road in your dream car or holding the keys to your new home. Picture yourself shaking hands with the customer who purchased your first painting or meeting someone you admire for the first time. Make sure that you attach intense positive feelings to your visualization. Anything we believe with emotion seems more real.

Affirmations can be useful when we are working toward taking a risk and stepping out of our comfort zone. Once we decide what risk we want to take, we can visualize the event in our minds first. We can vividly visualize achieving our desired result. We can feel the rush of exhilaration and the feelings of accomplishment that result from stepping out of our comfort zone. When we can visualize in our minds what we truly want, our thoughts begin to create that reality.

Affirmations, Intentions, and Goals

Affirmations, intentions, and goals are all very useful in creating the life that we really want to live. They are not the same, but they all support one another. Affirmations are visualizations which create a direction for attraction. They express what we really want to achieve and help create a visual scenario where we act as if we have already received our desired result. Affirmations support us in vividly honing our thoughts to align with our desired state of being. They help us get clear on exactly what results we want to gain and how we want to feel. Affirmations define our desired outcome or state of being. They specify what we really want.

Once we are clear on what we want, we can begin to align our actions with what we desire to achieve. When we desire to achieve something, we commit our thoughts and actions through intention. Our commitments create intentions and intentions inspire action. Remember, intentions are action statements that support affirmations. Intentions contain a verb and require us to do something that moves us closer to our desired state of being. Intentions are commitments to taking action. Goals are specific markers or signposts to achieve that support the intention or overall way of being. Here is an example:

Affirmation:

"I am surrounded by deep and loving friendships."

This is a state of being that you desire to have and through affirmations, you are making a statement as if what you desire is already yours. You are affirming that it is already coming to you or it is already here. Affirmations are stated in the present and usually being with "I am" or "I have". You can visualize anything your heart desires. You can visualize in your mind feeling happy, feeling loved, and being surrounded by meaningful friendships.

Intention:

"I am willing to create deep and loving relationships by being open and reaching out to others."

An intention is an *action* you are willing to take that will help you create your desired state of being. You created a desired state of being through your affirmation and visualization. Intention is a choice to show up in the world taking action in a specific way or demonstrating certain behaviors. Intentions always include a verb and require you to take action that is in alignment with your desired state of being. Intentions require you to do something. Intentions support affirmations and goals support intentions. With this intention, your action is *reaching out to others* which helps create what you desire in your affirmation, *loving friendships.*

Goals:

Call my friends once per week instead of waiting for them to call me.

Make time to talk openly about my feelings.

Forgive the past.

Goals are specific action steps or signposts to achieve that move you closer to your desired state of being. They are steps in the overall process of acting on your intention.

Attraction and Action

We can only attract what we truly want in life if we are able to master our fears and face the obstacles that are holding us back. Once we master our fears, we can access our authentic self and live as the joyful, peaceful, exuberant person our soul intended us to be. We can live each day as the whole, complete, unique, gifted person that we truly are. If we choose to sit back and revel in our judgment, blame, and righteousness, we cannot create a life that lives up to our potential. If we live our life in fear, then we cannot readily access love and trust. Before we can attract what we truly want in our life, we must build a strong personal foundation. We must be willing to look within ourselves first and uncover the fears that are keeping us from living our best life. Let's bring all of the tools and principles together.

As we have talked about, all of our reality starts with a thought, an image, or a vision in our mind. We cannot control every circumstance we are faced with but, we can control our responses. Therefore, what we experience in our outer world is a reflection of our inner thoughts and beliefs. If any part of our life is unsatisfactory to us, we must look within for answers. We can only create the life of our dreams by looking internally at our thoughts, feelings, and responses, instead of externally at the world around us. We change our lives by changing ourselves, not by wanting others to change. We change our lives by really looking at our motivations: are we motivated by fear and lack of trust in ourselves or are we motivated by love, authenticity, and self-trust? Are we motivated to take action in order to be accepted or are we motivated to take action because it comes from our heart, our inner wisdom, and a genuine desire to contribute to the world in a loving way?

What if someone says something that is very hurtful and we do not feel very loving? We always have choices. We can look within ourselves and consider if all or part of what they are saying is true. It might be true that we are reacting out of fear by feeling jealous, judgmental, defensive, or controlling. Maybe it is true or maybe it is not. It is up to us to look inside for the answers. We can also choose to reject another's opinion as false because it does not align with what we know our truth to be. When we are reactive to someone else, we must ask ourselves, "How much control over my feelings and my life do I want to give this person or this situation? How can I take charge of my life?"

In order to attract what we really want, we must take full responsibility for our lives in every way. We must release expectations that give away our power and keep us blaming and complaining. We must take responsibility to express our needs, our values, and ask for what we want instead of expecting everyone to live by our rule book. We are only in charge of ourselves and when we get stuck in our negative emotions, it is a call to action to take personal responsibility for our lives and our choices.

> *Negative emotions are a call to action to look within and decide how to be responsible for your own happiness.*

It is our responsibility to make choices that move us closer to living our best life and accessing our inner wisdom. We do this by acting on our commitments instead of our emotions. We each have an internal compass that guides us to act with integrity and to act in alignment with our highest values and beliefs. When we commit to acting on our intentions, we are proactive instead of reactive. We are in charge of our choices and we are in charge of our lives.

We must be willing to risk stepping outside of our comfort zone to learn about ourselves. Only through risk can we discover the depths of our abilities, talents, and skills. Only through risk can we learn what we are truly capable of achieving. Only through risk can we build confidence. There is nothing more powerful or fulfilling than pushing ourselves beyond what we thought we were capable of! The slightest step forward is immeasurably more rewarding than the best excuse for remaining stagnant.

As we take risks and fear reminds us that we are stepping outside of our comfort zone, we will feel unsure of ourselves. We may even misstep, but we must remember to be compassionate with ourselves because we are in the process of moving through our own personal evolution. We are in the process of learning, growing, and stretching. Through compassion, we learn to embrace our own humanity and the humanity in others. We learn how to see others in the process of their own evolution and we learn how to forgive. Once we can see ourselves with compassion, we open the doors to uncovering our authentic self. We can let go of our feelings of rejection and trust that the person we were born to be has always been there, waiting to shine.

When we have compassion, we no longer condemn ourselves and feel the sting of failure. Instead we see that life is unfolding perfectly in order for us to learn new skills. Life is happening perfectly in order to teach us exactly what we need to know in order to fulfill our potential. Each time we face adversity or challenge, we gain gifts from the experience. Adversity helps us to see that there is no wrong path, only paths that teach us different skills.

As we move along a path striving to reach a goal, we must choose to celebrate and acknowledge our forward progress. Focusing only on what is left undone can cause us to feel overwhelmed or unmotivated. When we give ourselves credit for all that we are and we all that we do, we can begin to see all of the great attributes that we each have that make us unique. We can stop attaching to a specific outcome that we think will make us feel fulfilled. We can let go of our need for perfection and strive instead for excellence. We can see the journey of our life as our true reward.

We can stop resisting and accept the truth of whatever comes our way in life. Life teaches us to bend and be flexible enough to face both opportunity and adversity equally. Whatever happens, we can handle it with integrity and honesty. We can proactively communicate and create meaningful connections with all of the people in our lives, without judgment, blame, or accusation. Building the types of relationships our heart's desire becomes easy when we choose to show up authentically.

We can choose to look at our lives with gratitude for everything that is good and see the world as for us instead of against us. There is always a choice. We can stop struggling and being pessimistic. We can see the abundance in our every day lives. There are gifts all around us every moment of every day if we choose to see them. We learn that some of the greatest gifts come when we share our knowledge, appreciation, and love with others. Giving to others is really giving to ourselves. Appreciating all that life has to offer is living in gratitude.

We can access the power of the Law of Attraction more readily when we can act as our authentic self. Our authentic self is the person we are meant to be without the roadblocks and barriers of our fears. Our fear is what stops us from being all that we can be. Our fear wants us to stay exactly where we are so that we always stay safe inside our comfort zone, but our comfort zone is truly the enemy of our creativity, our brilliance, and our possibilities. Our fearful self is not our authentic self; our fearful self is not who we truly are.

Our fearful self:

Judges... Blames... Condemns... Complains... Whines... Defends... Angers easily.... Isolates self... Seeks approval from others... Makes excuses... Talks negatively... Tries to be perfect... Lives in denial... Feels self-righteous... Gossips or thrives on drama... Worries... Feels guilty... Assumes the worst... Avoids facing the issues... Compares to others... Numbs self with addictions...Takes things personally...Lashes out at others... Talks condescendingly... Withholds love... Avoids personal responsibility... Sees self as a victim... Forecasts negative outcomes... Sees limits in life... Reviews the past over and over...Fears the future... Fears taking risks... Fears vulnerability and emotional transparency... Fears failing... Fears looking foolish... Fears being wrong... Fears rejection... Fears not being enough...

In contrast, our authentic self:

Feels at peace... Respects self and own needs...Welcomes growth and change... Sees opportunity and possibility... Steps out of comfort zone and risks... Is willing to be vulnerable... Feels a sense of significance and purpose when sharing who they are... Detaches from outcomes and enjoys the journey... Takes responsibility for their own thoughts, feelings, and actions... Releases the desire to decide how others should live... Feels responsible for creating their life experiences... Sees a vast array of choices... Relies on integrity as an internal compass... Feels emotions, but acts on commitments... Gives compassion to self and others... Forgives... Rejects rejection of self... Sees life as a journey of growth... Has an attitude of gratitude... Celebrates each step forward... Gives self credit... Communicates openly with flexibility... Feels self-trust... Wants to lift others up and see them excel... Accepts all of life without resistance... Feels empowered to live their best life...

> *When we commit to acting on our intentions, we are proactive instead of reactive. Even when life throws us a curve ball, we can choose to align our actions with our intentions instead of reacting to our emotions.*

The Law of Attraction

The Law of Attraction affirms that your life is created by your thoughts. The Law of Attraction states that your dominant thoughts determine what you attract to your life. It is almost as if you are a living magnet and your thoughts are the energy source. Everything that happens in your life, you are attracting with your thoughts. Like attracts like. So, who do you want to be when you are attracting energy to your life: your fearful self or your authentic self?

You choose your thoughts and the energy of your thoughts attracts events, circumstances, and people to your life. The attraction goes where our energy flows. If you think positive thoughts, you will attract positive effects. Conversely, focusing on negative outcomes will bring you just that. We are either using it to attract more peace, connection, and abundance or we are using it to create more disharmony, chaos, and lack in our lives. The Law of Attraction has been around since the beginning of time and it is ever present in all of our lives.

All energy is neutral until it is given direction. It does not differentiate between being used in a positive way or a negative way. It can be used to light an illegal drug house or a hospital. The same thing happens with the energy of our thoughts. Our thoughts decide the direction and flow of our energy. Each of our thoughts has a frequency and we attract all things to us that are on the same frequency as our thoughts. We decide the thoughts we think and therefore, we decide the frequency and direction of our energy. Our friends, our relationships, our job, our challenges, and our opportunities have all been attracted to us by our thoughts. If we are to harness the power of attraction in an empowering way, we must focus on what we want to attract to our life. Conversely, we can also attract exactly what we do not want if that is where we focus our thoughts.

Most of us have a very clear image of what we do not want. We do not want stress. We do not want pain. We do not want financial problems. We do not want to get fired or laid off from our jobs. We do not want to be judged or criticized or laughed at or blamed. We do not want to feel rejected, guilty, victimized, or bitter. We want to avoid these things. Yet, when our thoughts focus on these things, we are creating a higher probability that they will happen. When our thoughts are consumed by thinking about what we do not want, we are attracting more of what we do not want to our lives. Again, fear often plays a role. When we obsess about what we do not want instead of what we do want, our energy is pulling those negative events right to us.

The Law of Attraction can only give you what you focus on because the focus of your thoughts gives the energy direction. The energy does not differentiate between "I do not want" and "I do want". If we focus on criticism, judgment, and pain, that is what we are attracting to ourselves. The focus of the energy is what we attract. When our dominant thoughts are on how stressed and overwhelmed we feel, we are not attracting peace and serenity. We have not focused on peace and serenity. We have only focused on stress, so we are attracting *more* stress to our lives. We are actually blocking the things we desire because of our thoughts and focus. Thinking over and over about a shortage of money validates that we will have the reality of a shortage of money. Our thoughts can block abundance from coming to us. The desperate feeling of needing money comes from fear based thinking. The focus of thought is on lack, not abundance.

Our reality is a mirror reflection of our thoughts. If we focus on how we cannot find love, find a job, get a promotion, or achieve our goals, we are creating our reality through our dominant thoughts. If we worry and worry because we do not want something to happen, we are increasing the likelihood of it happening through the energy of our thoughts. The Law of Attraction gives you what you think about and it does not understand requests stated in the negative. "Don't" and "not" are not heard.

Here are some examples of what I mean.

The thought is:	Attraction hears:
I don't want to get stuck in traffic.	Get stuck in traffic
I don't want to be passed over at work.	Be passed over
I do not want get sick.	Get sick
I do not want be disrespected.	Be disrespected

On the other hand, if our dominant thoughts are on what we do want, we will attract those things to our life. Our thoughts are like seeds. The harvest depends on the seeds we plant. In nature, if we plant corn, then we will harvest corn. If we plant spinach, we will harvest spinach. And so it goes in our lives. Our dominant thoughts will determine what we harvest. Every thought we have creates our future reality. Replace negative thoughts of what you do not want to happen with positive thoughts of what you desire.

> Our thoughts are like seeds. The harvest depends on the seeds we plant. Our dominant thoughts determine what we will harvest.

There are four basic keys to attracting what your desire.

Four Key Steps to Attraction:

1. Decide what you want and ask for it.
2. Believe that it is achievable.
3. Remain constant in your desire.
4. Take Action in alignment with your desires.

Ask for What You Want

First and foremost, get very clear on what you do want. You cannot receive what you want until you decide what you want. You must believe that there will always be an ample supply. Focus clearly and concisely on what you *DO* want and state it in the present. I am in a loving, supportive relationship. I am being chosen to head up a special project at work. I am taking a cruise to the Mexican Riviera. I am fit and healthy. Keep your energy focus in the positive, not the negative. View life as an abundant journey. There is abundance for all who seek it. When you develop the skill to control your thoughts, you begin to control the effects and conditions that result from those thoughts. Changing your inner thoughts changes your external reality. If your thoughts are of fear, replace them with courage. If you thoughts are of failure, replace them with experience and success.

Create an image of what you want that is very specific and detailed. What do you want to achieve or gain? What is your dream? See it in your mind. If you want a home, build it in your mind. If your dream is about a career, envision yourself doing the job you love. What does the environment look like? What sounds do you hear? What emotions are you feeling when you envision receiving what you want? Who are the people that are around you? What qualities do they possess? What do you look like in your vision? What colors do you see? Make your vision as vivid as possible.

Describe your dream out loud. You can choose who you want to be, what you want to do, and what you want to have by focusing your thoughts. Your thoughts will create your reality. Remember we cannot attach to a specific timeline or a specific outcome. Life is happening perfectly in order to help us learn to live our best life. Please know that creating the life of our dreams is more than attracting material things to our lives. A fulfilling life includes many gifts that cannot be seen with the eyes, but only appreciated with the heart.

Believe that it is Achievable

If we truly believe that something is possible, we can visualize it happening in our mind's eye, and we are willing to make room for it in our lives, we can call forth the energy to create it. I stated before that our energy is neutral. It does not discriminate or differentiate positive from negative. Therefore we choose to give our energy direction through our thoughts. Thought is the most powerful, creative force known to man. Every achievement in business, literature, medicine, and science began with a thought. In early times, the power of electricity existed, but had not yet been harnessed. Man needed to believe it was possible in order to utilize it. Every thought is evaluated by our conscious minds. Our conscious minds evaluate whether we can accept something as true or view it as false. If we do not believe something is possible, we will not be able to focus our thoughts on it. An underlying belief that what we want is not possible can derail the Law of Attraction.

Whenever doubtful thoughts come into our mind, choose to move the focus of the thoughts into a positive. Tell yourself that whatever you can conceive with your mind, you can achieve. Belief is an important step in attracting what you want to your life. You must be willing to consider that you do not have to do things the way they have been done before.

You can creatively think of new ways. You can think out of the box. You can learn from your predecessor's experience, but you must be willing to believe that you can also forge your own way. Any limits in our thinking are self imposed and you can only attract what you believe is possible. Your thoughts have infinite power. It is like the old saying, "When there is a will, there is a way".

Say you buy a lottery ticket and you learn that you have the winning ticket because you have matched it to the numbers in the newspaper. At first, you experience disbelief and you check the numbers again. It dawns on you that you have really won! You jump up and down. Your heart is filled with exuberance. You call your closest friends and family. And then you start making plans in your mind about how you will start to spend the money. Technically, you do not have the money in your hands. Yet, you believe without a doubt that the money is yours. You do not spend it until it is placed in your bank account, but there is no doubt in your mind whatsoever that it will be there.

This is belief. This is the kind of belief that we can create in order to attract what our heart desires to our lives. We can create the feelings that come with getting what we want. We can feel the joy, the gratitude, and excitement of an abundant world. We must not attach to a specific date, time, or amount, but we move forward knowing that the Law of Attraction is at work.

I will give you another analogy. I am sure you have heard the story of the genie in the lamp. In the story, when the owner of the lamp rubbed the lamp, a magical genie appeared to grant three wishes. In our analogy, the lamp represents our thought and the genie represents the energy of our subconscious mind. In order for the energy of our subconscious mind to attract what we desire, we must first believe it is possible. If you have the lamp in your possession, but you do not believe in its powers, you will not waste your time rubbing it. On the other hand, if you understand the power of the lamp and believe in it, you will choose to rub it. You will choose to take action to acquire what you desire by rubbing the lamp. So, when you choose to believe that your dreams are possible and you decide to take action to move forward, you attract what you want through the Law of Attraction. You believe that your subconscious mind has the power to create anything.

We can choose to dream big or dream small. We can choose to focus on having just enough to get by or we can choose to focus on an ample amount. The Law of Attraction does not differentiate between the size or volume of the dream. It takes just as much energy and focus to do either. So, dream big. Believe that anything is possible for you. Do not feel like you are taking something away from someone else by dreaming big. The Universe offers everything to everyone and we must be willing to embrace it.

Remain Constant in Your Desire

Do not allow outside conditions, road blocks, or obstacles deter your focus. Discipline yourself to think, feel, speak, and behave your way toward achievement of your desires. Thinking negative thoughts of jealously, anger, and fear shifts your focus away from your desired result and acts like a boomerang. Getting stuck in disempowering expectations and emotions will block what you want to attract. Release resistance and accept "what is" before you at any given moment.

Emotions are a mirror of our thoughts. Our minds are constantly thinking whether we are conscious of our thoughts or not. How do we tell if we are thinking empowering thoughts? How do we tell if we are attracting what we want to our lives? Our emotions are the barometer of our thoughts. If we notice we are feeling angry or frustrated, our thoughts are focused on an expectation of a situation or a person. When we feel guilty, worried, or impatient, we are experiencing a disempowering emotion. Disempowering emotions are a call to action to do something differently: to see the situation in a new way, to take action in a new direction, to learn something, to see a gift in the experience, or to find gratitude. Just as our conditions are a result of our thoughts, so are our emotions. When we think a new thought, our emotions follow. It is impossible to feel bad while thinking a positive thought. Positive thoughts and emotions occur together as do negative thoughts and emotions. It is impossible to hate when you focus on love.

Pay attention to any actions that can shift your feelings and thoughts from negative to positive. I have said over and over that our emotions are a guide. They let us know how we are feeling and what we are thinking. We cannot feel sad while thinking happy thoughts. We must be thinking sad thoughts if we are feeling sad. Part of being human is experiencing a variety of emotions. Yet, it is not productive to get stuck in negative emotions for long periods of time. Negative emotions are a call to action letting us know that our thoughts are focusing on negative outcomes, pessimism, or malevolence. If we want to attract positive experiences, we must focus our energy and thoughts in a positive way.

Since we all are unique, the actions we can take to move into a positive state of mind will be different for each of us. I have noticed in my own life that different actions work at different times. If I am at home, I read my Gift and Gratitude Journal, listen to my favorite music, play games with my dog, give my kids a hug, take a bubble bath, or take time to be creative. If I am out in the world, I choose to participate fully, give a compliment, introduce myself to someone new, or take some other risk in order to energize myself and find my joy. Making random acts of kindness or giving of myself to another person without expectations also inspires me. It is the small, simple moments of joy that create a rewarding life. What actions can you use to inspire you at any given moment to move from negative thoughts to positive thoughts?

Here are some examples that can move you to a positive state of mind. Please feel free to add your own.

Actions that Manifest Positive Thoughts and Feelings

Listen to music	Give a compliment
Accept a compliment	Take a bubble bath
Sing with the radio	Connect with nature
Re-connect with an old friend	Send a thank you note
Jump in with both feet	Love a pet
Donate blankets to a shelter	Say an affirmation
Pray	Show gratitude
Make plans to be with friends	Exercise
Commit to act on intentions	Meditate
See miracles around you	Breathe deeply
Step out of your comfort zone	Appreciate art
Give a hug	Dance
Jump up and down	Seek knowledge
See wonder in your life	Ask questions
Give yourself credit	Pamper yourself
Express yourself	Celebrate action
Find humor in life	Simplify
Focus on the next step	Be a Lovecat!
Pick flowers to give away	Smell the roses
See the gifts in adversity	Show compassion
Take a break	Go for a walk
Trust your truth	Appreciate others

Positive Language

Our language is also a reflection of our thoughts and feelings. Have you ever had one of those days where everything seemed to go wrong? You say, "What an awful day". The next thing you know, something else goes wrong. You say, "What next? What else could happen to make this day worse?" Something else goes wrong because you have attracted something else to make your day worse. When you find yourself in this mode, use it as a wake up call to change your vocabulary. Words are verbal expressions of our thoughts. Change your language to attract more abundance and positive energy to your life.

Negative Language	Positive Language
I am confused	I seek clarity
I can't do it	I can do my best
I am overwhelmed	I am peaceful
I feel stupid	I seek knowledge
Problems are everywhere	I seek solutions
Life is hard	Life strengthens me
I am impatient	I am patient
My relationship is boring	I choose to be interesting
My ex is a jerk	I focus on my growth
You owe me	I give to myself
I am dumb	I am gifted
I feel under valued	I trust my worth
I feel foolish	I learn lessons
I see weaknesses	I appreciate strengths
I regret	Next time, I will choose

I'm drowning in debt	I focus on prosperity
I will never have money	I know prosperity is mine
I feel old and sick	I see the gifts of my body
I fear life	I love and embrace life
It is not possible	I can create anything I believe

Take Action in Alignment with Your Desire

Set intentions committing your thoughts, words, and deeds toward attracting what you want. The Principles of Intention and The Law of Attraction can work synergistically together. Remember, intention is what we are willing to do and how we want to show up in the world. It is deciding to make commitments and stand by them. When we stand by our commitments, our thoughts remain focused. We do not give ourselves permission to make excuses. Excuses block the Law of Attraction. When we make excuses, we create thoughts of doubt.

If you want to attract love into your life, then show love. An intention to show love might be "I am willing to show love to the people in my life through my words and actions". Be the kind of person that you want to attract to your life. Remember, like attracts like. If you want to find love, be more loving in your relationships. Learn how to authentically love yourself. Act as if you have love by making room in your life for a loving relationship.

If you want to attract more money or financial security, get rid of your thoughts of lack. Be grateful for what you have and focus your energy on abundance and wealth. Make choices and take actions that are in alignment with your intentions. If you need advice from a financial planner or debt consolidation consultant, seek it out. Take action. Creating an effective plan will support you in taking charge of your life which in turn, will enable you to think empowering thoughts.

If you want to lead a team, choose to embrace team work and leadership skills. Emulate leaders that you admire and respect. Ask if they are willing to be a mentor to you. Become an expert in seeking knowledge and leadership skill building. Practice leadership by leading your own life first and commit to standing by your integrity. Lead by example.

If you want to attract health and vitality to you life, set an intention that inspires you to live in a healthier way. You might say, "I am willing to eat foods that offer health benefits". Action must follow your thoughts. Feel gratitude for where you are and what you have. Then visualize where you want to be and see yourself interacting with health and vitality.

My personal intention when we relocated to North Carolina was, "I am willing to be open to moving to a place that is family oriented, close to nature, and brings me serenity." I bought a book on the fifty best places to raise a family, chose a location with my husband, and focused my thoughts. We faced challenges such as selling our former house in a depressed market. We went through a year of open houses on weekends. I worked diligently to get a transfer. Yet, my focus never wavered. I knew everything was happening as it was supposed to. A year later, job transfers to North Carolina were offered to us. I now see hills and trees. Our community is full of families and family oriented activities. My home brings me peace of mind and serenity. Intention and attraction helped me create the life I wanted. Our intentions solidify our thoughts and give our thoughts direction.

As you get clear on what you want and focus on attracting it to your life, opportunities will start to present themselves. You do not need to worry about knowing every single minutia of every action step ahead of time. A friend will invite you to a networking function. Just the right e-mail will show up in your inbox. A parking space will appear in a lot full of cars. You must be willing to take action on the opportunities as they are presented to you. You cannot allow fear to hold you back. Remember, fear wants you to stay safe. Action, risk, and attraction propel you forward toward the life you want to create. This action will feel inspiring. It may feel like you are stepping out of your comfort zone and you may be somewhat uncomfortable. Yet, you will feel a sense of excitement and passion to move forward because the action moves you closer to your heart's desire.

Even if you experience something that feels like failure, continue to move forward with your efforts because you are learning skills. Obstacles and challenges are simply opportunities to learn lessons. When they come along, they are a sign that there is something we need to learn. They let us know how to gain that information. There is no and can never be failure when you believe to the depths of your soul that something is possible for you. It can be darkest before the dawn, but the dawn always comes. Use your Gratitude Journal, see the gifts, and do not give up. Fill your mind with thoughts of determination, ambition, desire, and courage. Persevere and concentrate on what you want. Give yourself credit for each risk and each step forward. Act on your commitments. Make it fun and enjoy the journey. Your life is yours to create. Attract it and it will be yours. Remember, actions speak louder than words. Take action and break out of your comfort zone. Take Action for Life!

Action for Life Exercise

What do you really, really want? What are you willing to do today to make that happen?

Create a Dream Board. Cut out pictures of people you admire, places you want to go, and things you aspire to have in your life. I did this and my kids were amazed by the things I started drawing to my life! It is so much fun!

Think of 100 things you would like to accomplish. Create goals or action steps that you can take toward reaching your dreams. View it as an adventure and tackle one or two at a time.

Make a list of activities that move you from a negative state to a positive state. Make sure to use all of your tools to take charge of your thoughts and your life.

Each morning upon arising, choose to perform 10 minutes of mental house keeping. Find gratitude for the possibilities in the day ahead. Release negative thoughts. Act on your intentions. Give yourself credit.

Action for Life Team

Who has achieved something that you want to achieve? How can you learn from them?

Who could you ask to serve as a mentor to you?

People love to help others. Ask for help.

Who could you hire that has expertise to help you move forward? Could you utilize a Financial Planner, a Life Coach, or a Personal Trainer?

Chapter Strategy

Change your thoughts and change your life. Focus on positive energy, positive affirmations, living by intention, and achieving goals.

Chapter 10 Key Points

- The Law of Abundance tells us that whatever we can conceive in our minds through our visualizations, we can manifest in our life. When abundance comes, we must be willing to receive it. In order to maintain balance, we must also be willing to give back to the world with equal compensation.

- An affirmation is essentially a visualization of a desired state or outcome. Affirmations support thinking in the positive.

- The Law of Attraction is the law that states "like attracts like". We attract through our thoughts. We attract exactly what we focus our energy on. Positive attracts more positive. Negative attracts more negative.

- Intentions contain verbs and are a willingness to take action. Intentions reflect a commitment to showing up in the world in a specific way. They are a personal commitment to action. Intentions can support affirmations.

- Goals are specific action steps or benchmarks to achieve. Goals are most effective when they are specific, measurable, and attainable.

- Goals support intentions and intentions support affirmations. An affirmation might be seeing yourself already having your dream job; an intention might be committing to expanding the personal talents and skills that will better equip you for that job; and goals might be revising your resume, introducing yourself to a mentor, and finishing your degree. They all support one another.

- In my opinion, there are two primary forces that motivate people: fear and love. We are born to be loving beings and fear is the roadblock that stops us from living authentically.

- There are 4 Keys Steps to Attraction:

    Decide what you want and ask for it.

    Believe it is achievable.

    Remain constant in your desire.

    Take action in alignment with that desire.

- Choose actions and language that empower you to see the abundance in your life.